Afghan Splendor™

Afghan Splendor

CONTENTS

1. Red Hearts, Roses & Lace

2. Beginnings, Chicks & Bunnies

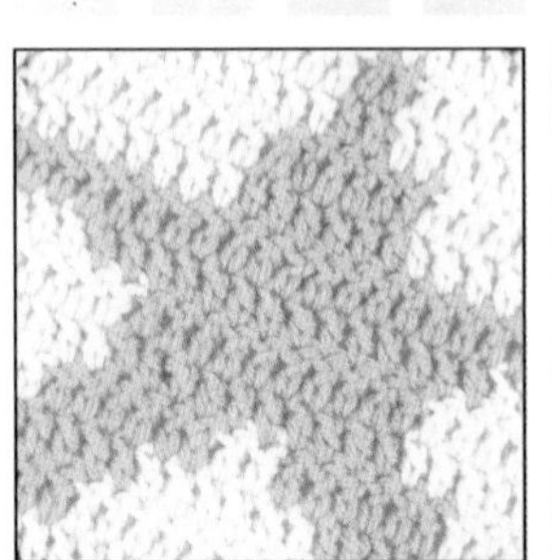

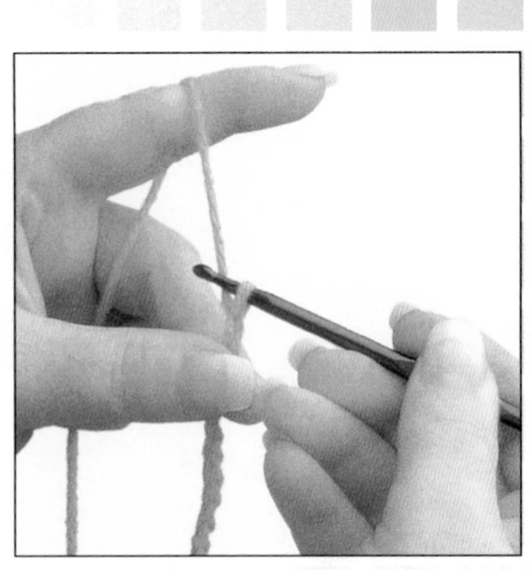

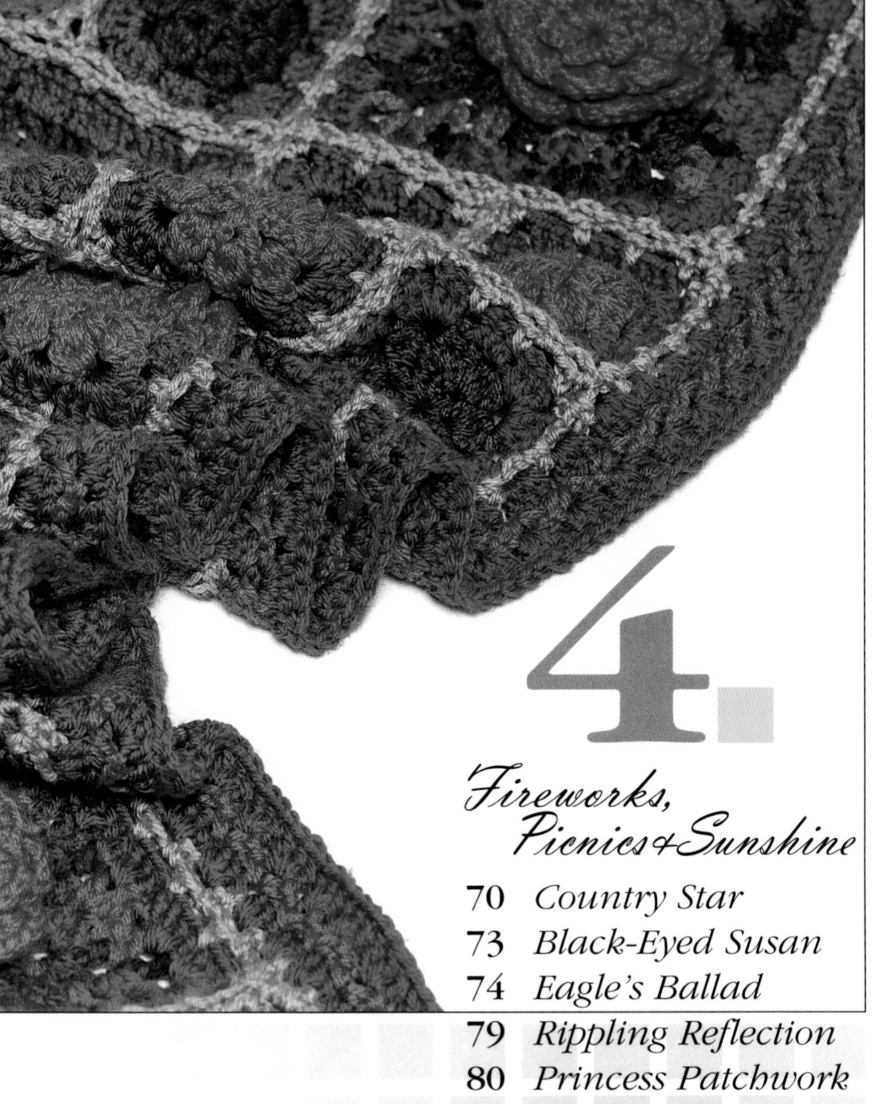

3. Mothers, Friends & Gardens

4. Fireworks, Picnics & Sunshine

5. Moonlight, Mischief & Magic

6. Harvest, Bounty & Family

7. Firesides, Snow & Mistletoe

Product Development Director
ANDY ASHLEY

Publishing Services Director
ANGE VAN ARMAN

Crochet Design Manager
DEBORAH LEVY-HAMBURG

Product Development Staff
MICKIE AKINS, DARLA HASSELL,
SANDRA MILLER MAXFIELD,
ALICE VAUGHAN,
ELIZABETH ANN WHITE

Senior Editor
DONNA SCOTT

Crochet Editorial Staff
SHIRLEY BROWN, LIZ FIELD,
SKEETER GILSON, SHARON LOTHROP,
NINA MARSH, LYNE PICKENS

Book Design
GREG SMITH

Graphic Artist/Supervisor
MINETTE COLLINS SMITH

Photography Manager
SCOTT CAMPBELL

Photographers
KEITH GODFREY,
TAMMY COQUAT-PAYNE,
ANDY J. BURNFIELD

Photo Stylist
MARTHA COQUAT

Color Specialist
BETTY HOLMES

Production Coordinator
GLENDA CHAMBERLAIN

Chief Executive Officer
JOHN ROBINSON

Marketing Director
SCOTT MOSS

Customer Service
1-800-449-0440

Pattern Services
(903) 636-5140

Library of Congress Cataloging-in-Publication Data
ISBN: 1-57367-111-8
First Printing: 2000
Library of Congress Catalog Card Number: 00-91850
Published and Distributed by
The Needlecraft Shop, Big Sandy, Texas 75755
Printed in the United States of America

Visit us at **NeedlecraftShop.com**

Dear Friends,

When I checked for words that were synonymous with splendor, I unearthed a wealth of descriptive terms. Grandeur centers around the first formal college dance I attended, wearing all of my sparkling finery while hoping I didn't trip over my 2" heels. Stateliness describes the feelings I recall as I walked across the stage to accept my diploma, again without the tripping.

Exquisiteness brings to memory the first time I held my niece, Ashley, nearly fifteen years ago. I especially like the expression spellbound. That word reminds me of my reaction the first time I set eyes upon my husband-to-be, Charles.

All of these words effortlessly roll into one big enough to encompass the variety, beauty and techniques demonstrated among the afghans that grace these pages. That one word can only be.....splendiferousness!

Donna

Red Hearts, Roses & Lace

Chapter One

1.

- Rose Arbor
- Loving Warmth
- Blush Rose
- Redwork Hearts
- Country Rose
- Pretty In Pink
- Sweet Baby Kisses

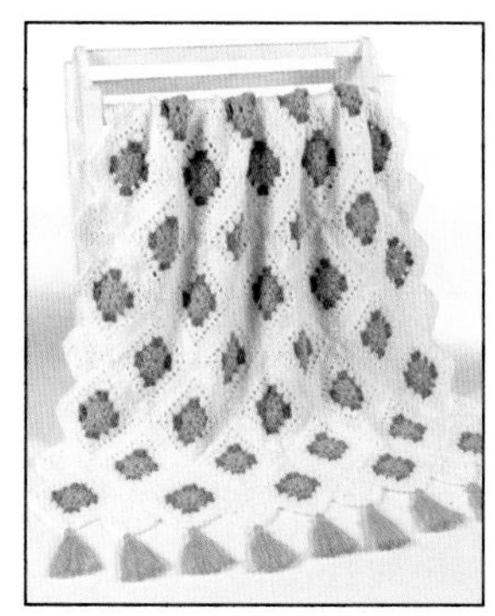

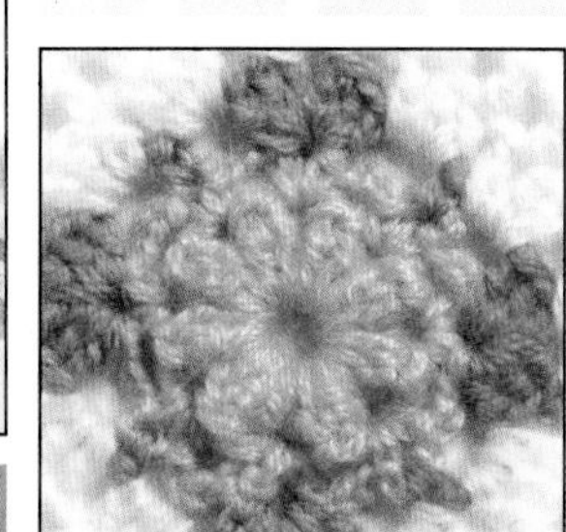

Afghan Splendor

Lavishly bordered with textured leaves, roses run rampantly across, welcoming the cool breeze.

Rose Arbor

by CAROL ALEXANDER
for CROCHET TRENDS & TRADITIONS

SIZE: 50" x 62".

MATERIALS: 3-ply worsted-weight yarn — 47 oz. black, 12 oz. each off-white and green, 7 oz. pink; tapestry needle; G and H crochet hooks or sizes needed to obtain gauges.

GAUGES: With **G hook,** rnds 1-6 of Block = $3\frac{3}{4}$" across. With **H hook,** 10 sts = 3". Each Block is 12" square.

SKILL LEVEL: ☆☆☆ Advanced

BLOCK (make 20)

Rnd 1: With G hook and pink, ch 4, sl st in first ch to form ring, ch 1, 16 sc in ring, join with sl st in first sc (16 sc).

Rnd 2: Ch 6, skip next st, (dc in next st, ch 3, skip next st) around, join with sl st in 3rd ch of ch-6 (8 dc, 8 ch sps).

Rnd 3: For **outer petals,** ch 1, (sc, 2 dc, ch 1, sl st in top of last dc made, 2 dc, sc) in each ch sp around, join with sl st in first sc (8 outer petals).

Rnd 4: For **first inner petal layer,** working in front of last rnd, (sc, 2 dc, ch 1, sl st in top of last dc made, 2 dc, sc) around post of each dc on rnd 2, join. Slide petals to top of dc posts.

Rnd 5: For **2nd inner petal layer,** working in front of last rnd around bottom of posts on same dc of rnd 2, (sc, hdc, dc, hdc, sc) around post of each dc around, join.

Rnd 6: For **center,** working in front of last rnd, sl st in skipped sc of rnd 1 directly below, ch 3, (sl st in next skipped sc of rnd 1, ch 3) around, join with sl st in first sl st, fasten off.

Rnd 7: With wrong side facing you, with G hook, join black with sc in **back bar** (see illustration) of 2nd dc on any outer petal, ch 3, (sc in **back bar** of 2nd dc on next outer petal, ch 3) around, join with sl st in first sc, **turn** (8 ch sps).

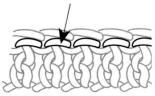

BACK BAR OF DC

Rnd 8: Sl st in first ch sp, ch 3, dc in same ch sp, ch 4, (2 dc in next ch sp, ch 4) around, join with sl st in top of ch-3.

***NOTES:** For **beginning puff stitch (beg puff st),** ch 3, (yo, insert hook in same sp, yo, draw up long lp) 2 times, yo, draw through 4 lps on hook, yo, draw through last 2 lps on hook.*

*For **puff stitch (puff st),** (yo, insert hook in ch sp, yo, draw up long lp) 3 times, yo, draw through 6 lps on hook, yo, draw through last 2 lps on hook.*

continued on page 11

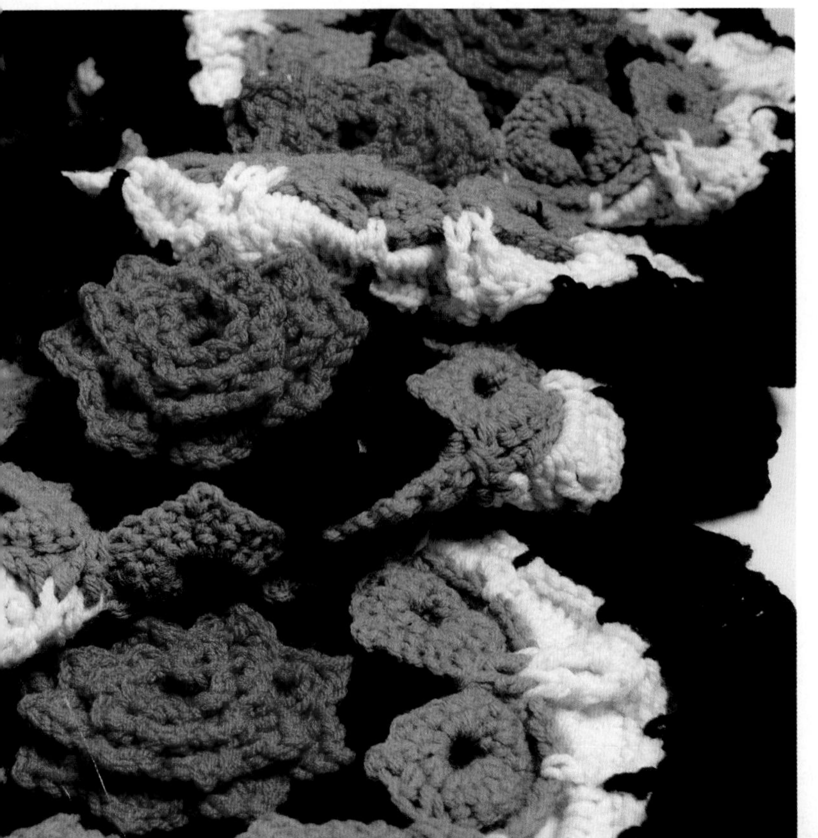

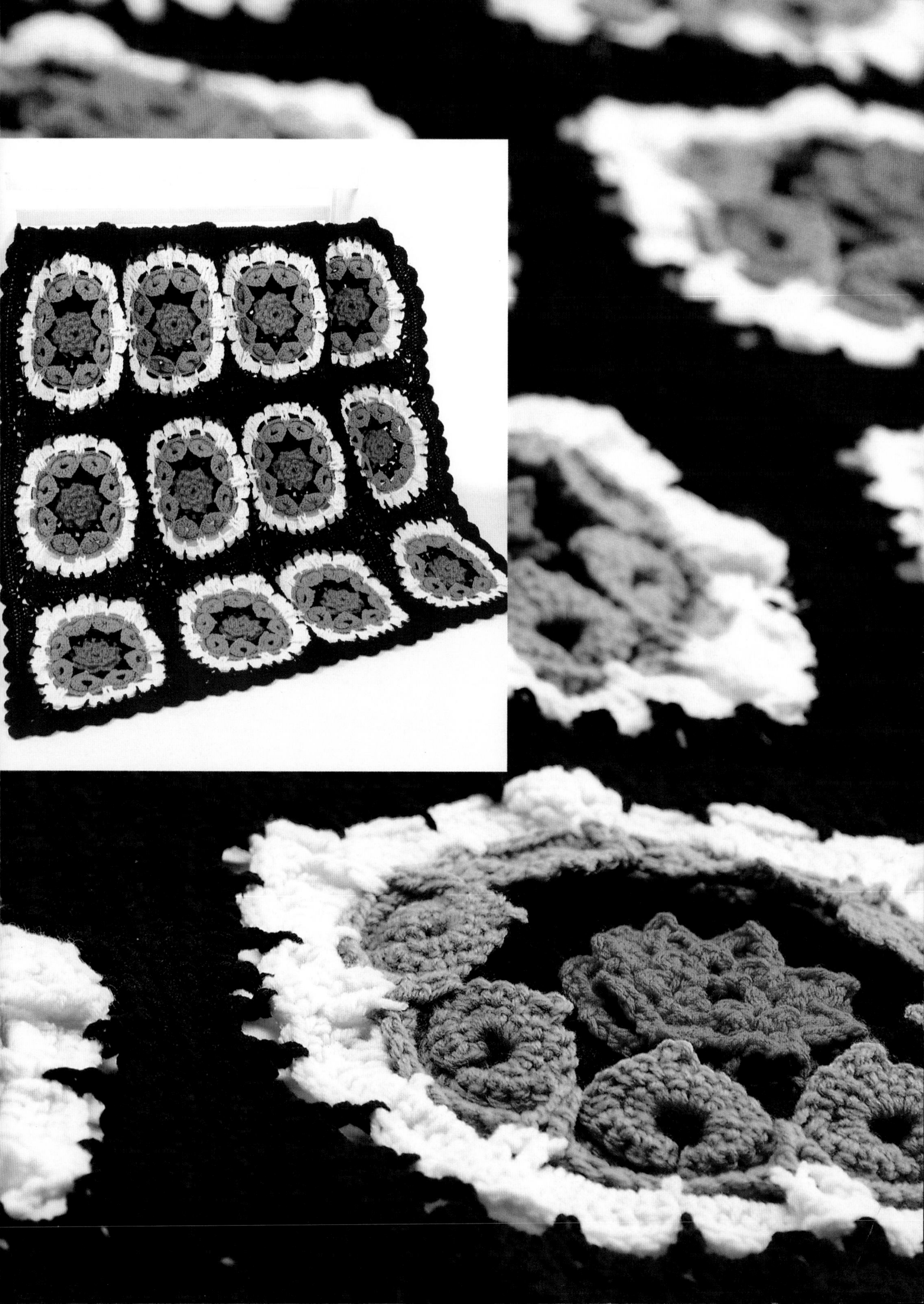

Crusades of soft shells, when combined with your own color scheme, are sure to add delightful appeal to any home decor.

Loving Warmth

by SANDRA JEAN SMITH
of SJS DESIGNS

SIZE: 47" x 73".

MATERIALS: Worsted-weight yarn — 48 oz. aran, 14 oz. green and 9 oz. rose; J crochet hook or size needed to obtain gauge.

GAUGE: 5 dc = 2"; 3 shells and 3 sl sts = 7"; 4 sl st rows and 4 shell rows = 5".

SKILL LEVEL: ☆☆☆ Advanced

CENTER

Row 1: With aran, ch 140, sc in 2nd ch from hook, sc in each ch across, turn (139 sc).

Row 2: Ch 3, dc in each st across, turn.

Row 3: Ch 1, sc in each st across, **do not** turn, fasten off.

***NOTES:** For **shell,** (3 dc, ch 1, 3 dc) in next st.*

*For **beginning half shell (beg half shell),** ch 3, 3 dc in same st.*

*For **ending half shell (end half shell),** 4 dc in last st.*

Row 4: Join aran with sl st in first st, (skip next 2 sts, shell in next st, skip next 2 sts, sl st in next st) across, **do not** turn, fasten off (24 sl sts, 23 shells).

Row 5: Join aran with sl st in first st, beg half shell, sl st in ch sp of next shell, (shell in next sl st, sl st in ch sp of next shell) across to last sl st, end half shell in last sl st, **do not** turn, fasten off (23 sl sts, 22 shells, 2 half shells).

Row 6: Join aran with sl st in first st, shell in next sl st, (sl st in next shell, shell in next sl st) across to last half shell, sl st in last dc of last half shell, **do not** turn, fasten off (24 sl sts, 23 shells).

Rows 7-43: Repeat rows 5 and 6 alternately, ending with row 5.

***NOTE:** For **decrease cluster (dec cl),** (yo, insert hook in next st, yo, draw lp through) 7 times, yo, draw through all 15 lps on hook.*

Row 44: Join aran with sc in first st, ch 2, dec cl, ch 2, (sc in next ch sp, ch 2, dec cl, ch 2) across to last st, sc in last st, **do not** turn, fasten off (46 ch-2 sps, 24 sc, 23 dec cls).

***NOTE:** First and last sl sts on following rnds are not used or counted as a st.*

Row 45: Working across 3 sides of outer edge, in ends of rows, join aran with sl st in row 3, ch 2, sc in same row, evenly space 64 more sc across, ch 2; working across last row, sc in each st and 2 sc in each ch sp across, ch 2; working in ends of rows, evenly space 64 sc across to opposite end of row 3, (sc, ch 2, sl st) in row 3, **do not** turn, fasten off (65 sc across each short end between ch-2 sps, 139 sc across long edge between corner ch-2 sps).

Row 46: Join aran with sl st in base of first st on

continued on next page

Loving Warmth

Continued from page 9

row 2, (dc, ch 2, dc) in first ch-2 sp on last row, dc in next 65 sts, (dc, ch 2, dc) in next ch-2 sp, dc in next 139 sts, (dc, ch 2, dc) in next ch sp, dc in next 65 sts, (dc, ch 2, dc) in next ch-2 sp, sl st in base of next st on row 2, **do not** turn, fasten off (67 dc across each short end between corner ch-2 sps, 141 dc across long edge between corner ch-2 sps).

Row 47: Join aran with sl st in first sc on row 1, sc in next st on last row, (sc, ch 2, sc) in next ch sp, sc in each st across with (sc, ch 2, sc) in each corner ch sp, sl st in last st on row 1, fasten off (69 sc across each short end between corner ch-2 sps, 143 sc across long edge between corner ch-2 sps).

BORDER

Rnd 1: Working around entire outer edge, join rose with sl st in first corner ch sp before bottom long edge, ch 5, dc in same sp, ch 1, skip next st, dc in next st; working in starting ch on opposite side of row 1, ch 1, skip next ch, (dc in next ch, ch 1, skip next ch) 69 times, dc in next st, ch 1, skip next st, *(dc, ch 2, dc) in next corner ch sp, ch 1, skip next st, (dc in next st, ch 1, skip next st) 34 times*, (dc, ch 2, dc) in next corner ch sp, ch 1, skip next st, (dc in next st, ch 1, skip next st) 71 times; repeat between **, join with sl st in 3rd ch of ch-5, fasten off (36 dc and 35 ch-1 sps across each short end between corner ch-2 sps, 73 dc and 72 ch-1 sps across each long edge between corner ch-2 sps).

Rnd 2: Join green with sc in first corner ch sp, ch 2, sc in same sp, *[sc in next st; (working in front of next ch-1 sp, dc in next skipped st on rnd before last, sc in next st on last rnd) across] to next corner ch-2 sp, (sc, ch 2, sc) in next corner ch-2 sp; repeat from * 2 more times; repeat between [ ], join with sl st in first sc (73 sts across each short end between corner ch-2 sps, 147 sts across each long edge between corner ch-2 sps).

Rnd 3: Sl st in next corner ch sp, ch 5, dc in same sp, *[ch 1, skip next st, (dc in next st, ch 1, skip next st) across] to next corner ch sp, (dc, ch 2, dc) in next corner ch sp; repeat from * 2 more times; repeat between [ ], join with sl st in 3rd ch of ch-5, fasten off (38 dc and 37 ch-1 sps across each short end between corner ch-2 sps, 75 dc and 74 ch-1 sps across each long edge between corner ch-2 sps).

Rnds 4-5: With rose, repeat rnds 2 and 3, ending with 40 dc and 39 ch-1 sps across each short end between corner ch-2 sps, 77 dc and 76 ch-1 sps across each long edge between corner ch-2 sps.

Rnd 6: Repeat rnd 2, fasten off (81 sts across each short end between corner ch-2 sps, 155 sts across each long edge between corner ch-2 sps).

Rnd 7: Join aran with sc in first corner ch sp, ch 2, sc in same sp, sc in each st around with (sc, ch 2, sc) in each corner ch sp, join with sl st in first sc (83 sc across each short end between corner ch-2 sps, 157 sc across each long edge between corner ch-2 sps).

Rnd 8: *Sl st in next corner ch sp, skip next st, shell in next st, skip next st, sl st in next st, (skip next 2 sts, shell in next st, skip next 2 sts, sl st in next st) across to last 3 sts on this side, skip next st, shell in next st, skip next st, sl st in next corner ch sp, skip next 2 sts, shell in next st, skip next 2 sts, (sl st in next st, skip next 2 sts, shell in next st, skip next 2 sts) across to next corner ch sp; repeat from *, join with sl st in first sl st (14 shells and 13 sl sts across each short edge between corner sl sts, 27 shells and 26 sl sts across each long edge between corner sl sts).

Rnd 9: Ch 3, (2 dc, ch 1, 3 dc) in same st, sl st in next shell, (shell in next sl st, sl st in next shell) around, join with sl st in top of ch-3.

Rnd 10: Sl st in each of next 2 sts, sl st in next ch sp, ch 1, sc in same sp, ch 2, dec cl, ch 2, (sc in next ch sp, ch 2, dec cl, ch 2) around, join with sl st in first sc.

Rnd 11: Ch 1, (sc, ch 2, sc) in first st, 2 sc in each ch sp and sc in each st around with (sc, ch 2, sc) in each corner sc, join (85 sc across each short end between corner ch-2 sps, 163 sc across each long edge between corner ch-2 sps).

Rnd 12: Ch 3, (2 dc, ch 2, 2 dc) in next corner ch sp, dc in each st around with (2 dc, ch 2, 2 dc) in each corner ch sp, join with sl st in top of ch-3 (89 dc across each short end between corner ch-2 sps, 167 dc across each long edge between corner ch-2 sps).

Rnd 13: Ch 1, sc in each st around with (2 sc, ch 2, 2 sc) in each corner ch sp, join with sl st in first sc, fasten off (93 sc across each short end between corner ch-2 sps, 171 sc across each long edge between corner ch-2 sps).

Rnd 14: Join rose with sl st in any corner ch sp, ch 5, dc in same sp, *[ch 1, skip next st, (dc in next st, ch 1, skip next st) across] to next corner ch sp, *(dc, ch 2, dc) in next corner ch sp; repeat from * 2 more times; repeat between [ ], join with sl st in 3rd ch of ch-5, fasten off

Rnds 15-16: Repeat rnds 2 and 3.

Rnd 17: With rose, repeat rnd 2, **turn.**

Rnd 18: Sl st in each st and in each ch around, join with sl st in first sl st, fasten off.◆

Rose Arbor

Continued from page 6

Rnd 9: Sl st in next st, sl st in next ch sp, beg puff st, ch 2, (puff st in same sp, ch 2) 2 times, (puff st, ch 2) 3 times in each ch sp around, join with sl st in top of beg puff st (24 puff sts, 24 ch sps).

Rnd 10: Ch 3, 2 dc in next ch sp, (dc in next st, 2 dc in next ch sp) around, join with sl st in top of ch-3 (72 dc).

***NOTE:** Keep yarn tension loose on the following rnds to prevent work from cupping.*

Rnd 11: Ch 1, sc in first st, ch 12, skip next 8 sts, (sc in next st, ch 12, skip next 8 sts) around, join with sl st in first sc, fasten off (8 ch sps).

***NOTE:** Use H hook for remainder of Afghan.*

Rnd 12: Join green with sc in any ch sp, 28 sc in same sp, ch 1, (29 sc in next ch sp, ch 1) around, join (232 sc, 8 ch sps).

Rnd 13: Ch 1, sc in first 12 sts, mark 5th st of 12-sc group, ch 1, *[(sc in next st, ch 1) 3 times; for **tip of leaf,** sc around side of last sc made; (sc in next st, ch 1) 3 times], sc in next 6 sts, ch 1; to **form leaf,** drop lp from hook, insert hook from front to back in last marked st bringing leaf forward, draw dropped lp through, ch 1; sc in next 5 sts on last rnd, skip next ch sp, sc in next 12 sts, mark 5th st of 12-sc group, ch 1; joining to last leaf made, drop lp from hook, insert hook from front to back in 3rd ch sp after tip of last leaf pushing sts in between to back, draw dropped lp through, ch 1; repeat from * 6 more times; repeat between [ ]; joining to first leaf, drop lp from hook, insert hook from back to front in 3rd ch sp before tip of first leaf, draw dropped lp through, ch 1, sc in next 6 sts on last rnd, ch 1; to **form leaf,** drop lp from hook, insert hook from front to back in last marked st bringing leaf forward, draw dropped lp through, ch 1; sc in last 5 sts on last rnd, join.

Rnd 14: Skipping leaves, ch 1, sc in first 4 sts, sc in ch sp of next leaf joining, (sc in next 9 sts, sc in ch sp of next leaf joining) around to last 5 sts, sc in last 5 sts, join (80 sc).

Rnd 15: Ch 1, sc in first 9 sts, work 2 tr in joining between next 2 leaves and in next st on last rnd at same time, (sc in next 9 sts, work 2 tr in joining between next 2 leaves and in next st on last rnd at same time) around, join, fasten off (88 sts).

Rnd 16: Join off-white with sc in 6th sc of any 9-sc group, ch 10, skip next 10 sts, (sc in next st, ch 10, skip next 10 sts) around, join (8 sc, 8 ch-10 sps).

***NOTE:** For **long double crochet (long dc),** yo, insert hook from front to back around post of specified st, yo, draw up long lp, (yo, draw through 2 lps on hook) 2 times.*

Rnd 17: Sl st in first ch sp, ch 2, (3 dc, 3 tr) in same sp, *[long dc around post of next tr on rnd before last, ch 3, long dc around post of next tr on rnd before last, (3 tr, 3 dc, hdc) in same ch sp on last rnd], (hdc, 3 dc, 3 tr) in next ch sp; repeat from * 6 more times; repeat between [ ], join with sl st in top of ch-2 (128 sts, 8 ch sps).

Rnd 18: *[Sc in next 5 sts, hdc in next st, skip next st, 3 hdc in next ch sp, skip next st, hdc in next st, sc in next 5 sts, ch 1, skip next st], sl st in next st; repeat from * 6 more times; repeat between [ ], join with sl st in joining sl st of last rnd, fasten off.

Rnd 19: Join black with sc in center st of any 3-hdc group, ch 4, sc in same st, [◊*ch 4, skip next 3 sts, sc in next st, ch 5, skip next 3 sts, skip next ch sp; working over next sl st, dc in next ch sp on rnd before last, ch 5, skip next 3 sts, sc in next st, ch 4, skip next 3 sts*, sc in next st; repeat between **◊, (sc, ch 4, sc) in next st]; repeat between [ ] 2 more times; repeat between ◊◊, join with sl st in first sc (8 ch sps across each side between corner ch sps).

***NOTE:** For **double treble crochet (dtr),** yo 3 times, insert hook in ch sp, yo, draw lp through, (yo, draw through 2 lps on hook) 4 times.*

Rnd 20: Sl st in first corner ch sp, ch 4, (tr, dtr, ch 2, dtr, 2 tr) in same sp, *[4 tr in next ch sp, (3 tr, dc) in next ch sp, (3 dc, hdc) in next ch sp, (hdc, 2 sc) in next ch sp, (2 sc, hdc) in next ch sp, (hdc, 3 dc) in next ch sp, (dc, 3 tr) in next ch sp, 4 tr in next ch sp], (2 tr, dtr, ch 2, dtr, 2 tr) in next corner ch sp; repeat from * 2 more times; repeat between [ ], join with sl st in top of ch-4 (36 sts across each side between ch sps).

Rnd 21: Ch 2, hdc in each of next 2 sts, (2 hdc, ch 2, 2 hdc) in next ch sp, *hdc in next 13 sts, sc in next 10 sts, hdc in next 13 sts, (2 hdc, ch 2, 2 hdc) in next ch sp; repeat from * 2 more times, hdc in next 13 sts, sc in next 10 sts, hdc in last 10 sts, join with sl st in top of ch-2 (40 sts on each side between corner ch sps).

Holding Blocks wrong sides together, matching sts, with black, sew together in 4 rows of 5 Blocks each.

BORDER

Rnd 1: Working around entire outer edge, join black with sl st in any corner ch sp, ch 3, (dc, ch 2, 2 dc) in same sp, dc in each st and in each ch sp on each side of seams around with (2 dc, ch 2, 2 dc) in each corner ch sp, join with sl st in top of ch-3 (170 dc across each short end between corner ch sps, 212 dc across each long edge between corner ch sps).

Rnd 2: Sl st in next st, sl st in next ch sp, ch 3, (2 dc, ch 2, 3 dc) in same sp, *[sl st in next st, hdc in next st, (dc in next st, 3 tr in next st, dc in next st, hdc in next st, sl st in next st, hdc in next st) across] to next corner ch sp, (3 dc, ch 2, 3 dc) in next corner ch sp; repeat from * 2 more times; repeat between [ ], join, fasten off.◆

Pretty popcorn roses, worked in double strand yarn, capture the senses while making an easy and elegant gift.

Blush Rose

by MAGGIE WELDON

SIZE: 52½" x 63" not including Tassels.

MATERIALS: Fuzzy worsted-weight yarn — 36 oz. white, 25 oz. pink and 8 oz. green; tapestry needle; H crochet hook or size needed to obtain gauge.

GAUGE: With **2 strands held together,** rnds 1 and 2 of Large Motif = 3¼" across. Each Large Motif is 7½" square. Each Small Motif is 4¼" square.

SKILL LEVEL: ☆☆ Average

***NOTE:** Use 2 strands same color yarn held together throughout.*

LARGE MOTIF (make 50)

***NOTES:** For **beginning popcorn (beg pc)**, ch 3, 3 dc in ring, drop lp from hook, insert hook in top of ch-3, draw dropped lp through.*

*For **popcorn (pc)**, 4 dc in ring, drop lp from hook, insert hook in first dc of 4-dc group, draw dropped lp through.*

Rnd 1: With pink, ch 6, sl st in first ch to form ring, beg pc, ch 2, (pc, ch 2) 7 times, join with sl st in top of beg pc (8 ch-2 sps).

Rnd 2: Sl st in next ch sp, ch 1, (sc, ch 3, sc) in same sp, ch 3, *(sc, ch 3, sc) in next ch sp, ch 3; repeat from * around, join with sl st in first sc, fasten off (16 ch-3 sps).

Rnd 3: Join green with sl st in first ch sp, ch 3, (2 dc, ch 2, 3 dc) in same sp, ch 3, skip next ch sp, sc in next ch sp, ch 3, skip next ch sp, *(3 dc, ch 2, 3 dc) in next ch sp, ch 3, skip next ch sp, sc in next ch sp, ch 3, skip next ch sp; repeat from * around, join with sl st in top of ch-3, fasten off (8 ch-3 sps, 4 ch-2 sps).

Rnd 4: Join white with sl st in any corner ch-2 sp, ch 3, (2 dc, ch 2, 3 dc) in same sp, 3 dc in next ch-3 sp, ch 1, 3 dc in next ch-3 sp, *(3 dc, ch 2, 3 dc) in next corner ch-2 sp, 3 dc in next ch-3 sp, ch 1, 3 dc in next ch-3 sp; repeat from * around, join (48 dc, 4 ch-2 sps, 4 ch-1 sps).

Rnd 5: Sl st in next st, ch 4, skip next st, *[(dc, ch 1, dc, ch 2, dc, ch 1, dc) in next ch-2 sp, ch 1, skip next st, (dc in next st, ch 1, skip next st or ch) across] to next corner ch-2 sp; repeat from * 2 more times; repeat between [ ], join with sl st in 3rd ch of ch-4 (40 dc, 36 ch-1 sps, 4 ch-2 sps).

Rnd 6: Working this rnd in **back lps** only, ch 3, dc in each st and in each ch around with (2 dc, ch 2, 2 dc) in each corner ch-2 sp, join with sl st in top of ch-3, fasten off.

SMALL MOTIF (make 18)

Rnd 1: With white, ch 4, sl st in first ch to form ring, ch 4, dc in ring, ch 3, (dc, ch 1, dc, ch 3) 3 times in ring, join with sl st in 3rd ch of ch-4 (8 dc,

continued on page 19

Baby, snuggled in her precious pink motif array, nods softly as she quietly slumbers the soundless night away.

Sweet Baby Kisses

by TRUDY ATTEBERRY

SIZE: 37" x 43".

MATERIALS: Baby yarn — 10 oz. white and 8 oz. pink; G crochet hook or size needed to obtain gauge.

GAUGE: Rnds 1 and 2 of Large Motif = 2" across. Each Large Motif is 6" across.

SKILL LEVEL: ☆☆ Average

FIRST ROW

First Large Motif

Rnd 1: With white, ch 6, sl st in first ch to form ring, ch 1, 16 sc in ring, join with sl st in first sc (16 sc).

Rnd 2: Ch 4, dc in same st, ch 1, skip next st, *(dc, ch 1, dc) in next st, ch 1, skip next st; repeat from * around, join with sl st in 3rd ch of ch-4 (16 ch-1 sps).

Rnd 3: Sl st in next ch sp, ch 2, (hdc, ch 1, 2 hdc) in same sp, sc in next ch sp, *(2 hdc, ch 1, 2 hdc) in next ch sp, sc in next ch sp; repeat from * around, join with sl st in top of ch-2 (40 sts, 8 ch-1 sps).

Rnd 4: Sl st in next st, ch 1, sc in same st, *[(3 dc, ch 1, 3 dc) in next ch sp, skip next st, sc in next st, skip next 2 sts], sc in next st; repeat from * 6 more times; repeat between [ ], join with sl st in first sc, fasten off (64 sts, 8 ch-1 sps).

Rnd 5: Join pink with sc in any ch sp, ch 2, sc in same sp, *[sc in each of next 3 sts, skip next 2 sts, sc in each of next 3 sts], (sc, ch 2, sc) in next ch sp; repeat from * 6 more times; repeat between [ ], join, fasten off.

Rnd 6: Join white with sc in any ch sp, ch 2, sc in same sp, *[ch 1, skip next st, sc in next st, ch 1, skip next st, sc next 2 sts tog, ch 1, skip next st, sc in next st, ch 1, skip next st], (sc, ch 2, sc) in next ch sp; repeat from * 6 more times; repeat between [ ], join, fasten off (40 sc, 32 ch-1 sps, 8 ch-2 sps).

Rnd 7: Join pink with sc in any ch-2 sp, ch 3, sc in same sp, *[ch 3, skip next sc, sc in next sc, ch 5, skip next sc, sc in next sc, ch 3, skip next sc], (sc, ch 3, sc) in next ch-2 sp; repeat from * 6 more times; repeat between [ ], join, fasten off (24 ch-3 sps, 8 ch-5 sps).

Second Large Motif

Rnds 1-6: Repeat same rnds of First Large Motif.

NOTES: *For **joining ch-3 sp,** ch 1, sl st in 2nd ch of corresponding ch-3 sp on other Motif, ch 1.*

*For **joining ch-5 sp,** ch 2, sl st in 3rd ch of corresponding ch-5 sp on other Motif, ch 2.*

Rnd 7: Join pink with sc in any ch-2 sp; joining

continued on next page

Sweet Baby Kisses

Continued from page 23

to side of last Large Motif (see Joining Diagram), work joining ch-3 sp, sc in same sp on this Motif, ch 3, skip next sc, sc in next sc, work joining ch-5 sp, skip next sc on this Motif, sc in next sc, ch 3, skip next sc, sc in next ch-2 sp, skip next ch-3 sp on other Motif, work joining ch-3 sp, sc in same sp on this Motif, *[ch 3, skip next sc, sc in next sc, ch 5, skip next sc, sc in next sc, ch 3, skip next sc], (sc, ch 3, sc) in next ch-2 sp; repeat from * 5 more times; repeat between [ ], join, fasten off.

JOINING DIAGRAM

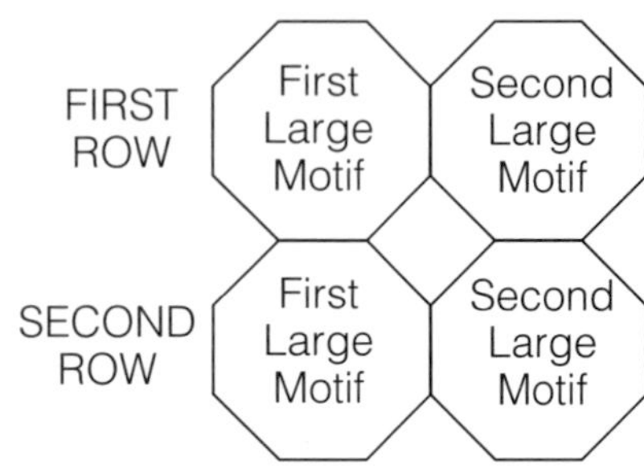

Repeat Second Large Motif 4 more times for a total of 6 Large Motifs on this row.

SECOND ROW

First Large Motif

Joining to bottom of First Large Motif on last row, work same as First Row Second Large Motif.

Second Large Motif

Rnds 1-6: Repeat same rnds of First Row First Large Motif.

Rnd 7: Join pink with sc in any ch-2 sp; joining to bottom of next Large Motif on last row, (work joining ch-3 sp, sc in same sp on this Motif, ch 3, skip next sc, sc in next sc, work joining ch-5 sp, skip next sc on this Motif, sc in next sc, ch 3, skip next sc, sc in next ch-2 sp, skip next ch-3 sp on other Motif, work joining ch-3 sp, sc in same sp on this Motif), ch 3, skip next sc, sc in next sc, ch 5, skip next sc, sc in next sc, ch 3, skip next sc, sc in next ch-2 sp; joining to side of last Large Motif on this row, repeat between ( ), *[ch 3, skip next sc, sc in next sc, ch 5, skip next sc, sc in next sc, ch 3, skip next sc], (sc, ch 3, sc) in next ch-2 sp; repeat from * 3 more times; repeat between [ ], join, fasten off.

Repeat Second Large Motif 4 more times for a total of 6 Large Motifs on this row.

Repeat Second Row 5 more times for a total of 7 Rows.

FILLER MOTIF

*NOTES: For **beginning popcorn (beg pc)**, ch 3, 3 dc in ring, drop lp from hook, insert hook in top of ch-3, draw dropped lp through.*

*For **popcorn (pc)**, 4 dc in ring, drop lp from hook, insert hook in first dc of 4-dc group, draw dropped lp through.*

Rnd 1: With pink, ch 4, sl st in first ch to form ring, beg pc, ch 2, (pc in ring, ch 2) 3 times, join with sl st in top of beg pc, fasten off (4 pc, 4 ch-2 sps).

Rnd 2: Join white with sl st in first st, ch 2, (2 dc, ch 2, 2 dc) in next ch sp, *hdc in next st, (2 dc, ch 2, 2 dc) in next ch sp; repeat from * around, join with sl st in top of ch-2 (20 sts, 4 ch-2 sps).

Rnd 3: Ch 1, sc in each st around with (sc, ch 2, sc) in each corner ch sp, join with sl st in first sc, fasten off.

Rnd 4: Join pink with sc in any ch sp; working in sps between Large Motifs, *[ch 1, sl st in joining sl st between Large Motifs, ch 1, sc in same sp on this Motif, ch 1, sl st in 2nd ch of next ch-3 sp on other Motif, ch 1, skip next 2 sts on this Motif, sc in next st, ch 1, sl st in 3rd ch of next ch-5 sp on other Motif, ch 1, skip next st on this Motif, sc in next st, ch 1, sl st in 2nd ch of next ch-3 sp on other Motif, ch 1, skip next 2 sts on this Motif], sc in next ch sp; repeat from * 2 more times; repeat between [ ], join with sl st in first sc, fasten off.

Repeat Filler Motif in each space between Large Motifs.

EDGING

*NOTE: For **scallop**, dc in next ch-5 sp, (ch 1, dc in same sp) 3 times.*

Join pink with sc in joining sl st between last 2 Large Motifs on one short end, ch 3, sc in same st, ◊•[ch 3, sc in next ch-3 sp, scallop in next ch-5 sp, sc in next ch-3 sp, ch 3, *(sc, ch 3, sc) in next ch-3 sp, ch 3, sc in next ch-3 sp, scallop in next ch-5 sp, sc in next ch-3 sp, ch 3*; repeat between **, (sc, ch 3, sc) in next joining sl st between Motifs]; repeat between [ ] across to last Motif on this side, ch 3, sc in next ch-3 sp, scallop in next ch-5 sp, sc in next ch-3 sp, ch 3; repeat between ** 4 more times•, (sc, ch 3, sc) in next joining sl st between Motifs; repeat from ◊ 2 more times; repeat between ••, join with sl st in first sc, fasten off.◆

Beginnings, Chicks & Bunnies

Chapter Two

2.

Blessed Moments
Baby's Color Wheel
Ice Cream Cones
Ribbons & Roses
Spring Breeze
Grape Vineyard
Lollipops

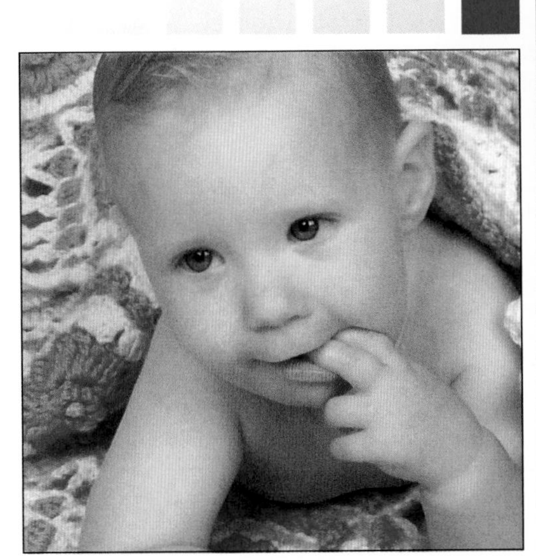

Afghan Splendor

May God's grace smile upon your spiritual journey wrapped in the warmth of this international symbol of His love.

Blessed Moments

by MAGGIE WELDON

SIZE: 47½" x 55½".

MATERIALS: Worsted-weight yarn — 35 oz. off-white, 11 oz. rose, 7 oz. navy; tapestry needle; H crochet hook or size needed to obtain gauge.

GAUGE: 7 sts = 2"; 4 sc rows = 1". Each Block is 11½" x 13½".

SKILL LEVEL: ☆☆ Average

BLOCK (make 16)

NOTES: *When changing colors (see page 159), always drop yarn to wrong side of work. Use a separate skein or ball of yarn for each color section.* ***Do not*** *carry yarn across from one section to another over more than 1 or 2 sts. Fasten off colors at end of each color section.*

Work odd-numbered graph rows from right to left and even-numbered rows from left to right.

Each square on graph equals one sc.

Row 1: With off-white, ch 36, sc in 2nd ch from hook, sc in each ch across, turn (35 sc).

Row 2: Ch 1, sc in each st across, turn.

Row 3: For **row 3 of graph** on page 31, ch 1, sc in first 16 sts changing to navy in last st made, sc in each of next 3 sts changing to off-white in last st made, sc in last 16 sts, turn.

Rows 4-48: Ch 1, sc in each st across changing colors according to graph, turn.

Rnd 49: Working around outer edge, ch 1, 3 sc in first st, sc in each st across with 3 sc in last st, (evenly space 44 sc across ends of rows); working in starting ch on opposite side of row 1, 3 sc in first ch, sc in each ch across with 3 sc in last ch; repeat between ( ), join with sl st in first sc, fasten off.

Rnd 50: Join rose with sl st in any st, ch 3, dc in each st around with (2 dc, ch 2, 2 dc) in each center corner st, join with sl st in top of ch-3, fasten off.

Holding Blocks wrong sides together, matching sts, with rose, sew together through **back lps** in 4 rows of 4 Blocks each.

BORDER

Working around entire outer edge, skipping seams, join rose with sl st in any st, ch 3, dc in each st and in each ch sp on each side of seams around with (2 dc, ch 2, 2 dc) in each corner ch sp, join with sl st in top of ch-3, fasten off.◆

continued on page 31

Entertain baby as popcorn stitches dance their way around festive motifs crocheted in dazzling color combinations.

Baby's Color Wheel

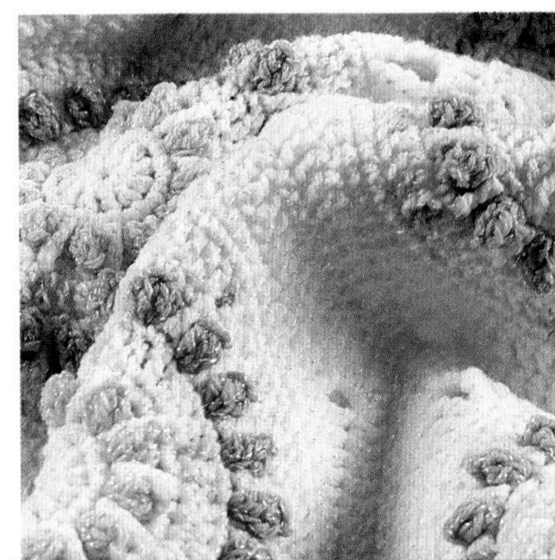

by ELLEN ANDERSON EAVES

SIZE: 44" x 45".

MATERIALS: Pompadour baby yarn — 14 oz. white, 5½ oz. lavender, 4 oz. variegated, 3½ oz. peach; tapestry needle; F crochet hook or size needed to obtain gauge.

GAUGE: Rnds 1 and 2 of Hexagon = 1½" across. Each Hexagon is 8" across.

SKILL LEVEL: ☆☆ Average

HEXAGON (make 22)

Rnd 1: With white, ch 4, 11 dc in 4th ch from hook, join with sl st in top of ch-3 (12 dc).

Rnd 2: Ch 1, 2 sc in each st around, join with sl st in first sc, fasten off (24 sc).

***NOTES:** For **beginning popcorn (beg pc)**, ch 3, 4 dc in same st, drop lp from hook, insert hook in top of ch-3, draw dropped lp through.*

*For **popcorn (pc)**, 5 dc in next st, drop lp from hook, insert hook in first st of 4-dc group, draw dropped lp through.*

Rnd 3: Join peach with sl st in any st, beg pc, dc in **back lp** of next st, (pc in **both lps** of next st, dc in **back lp** of next st) around, join with sl st in top of beg pc, fasten off (12 pc, 12 dc).

Rnd 4: Join white with sc in any pc, 2 sc in same st, tr in **front lp** of next st on rnd before last, skip next st on last rnd, (3 sc in next pc, tr in **front lp** of next st on rnd before last, skip next st on last rnd) around, join with sl st in first sc, fasten off (36 sc, 12 tr).

Rnd 5: Join variegated with sl st in any st, ch 3, dc in each st around, join with sl st in top of ch-3, fasten off (48 dc).

Rnd 6: Join white with sc in any st, sc in each st around, join with sl st in first sc, fasten off.

Rnd 7: Join lavender with sl st in any st, beg pc, 2 dc in **back lp** of next st, (pc in **both lps** of next st, 2 dc in **back lp** of next st) around, join with sl st in top of beg pc, fasten off (48 dc, 24 pc).

Rnd 8: Join white with sc in 2nd dc of any 2-dc group, sc in each of next 2 sts, tr in **front lp** of next st on rnd before last, (sc in each of next 3 sts on last rnd, tr in **front lp** of next st on rnd before last) around, join with sl st in first sc, fasten off (72 sc, 24 tr).

Rnd 9: Join variegated with sl st in any st, ch 3, dc in each st around, join with sl st in top of ch-3, fasten off.

Rnd 10: Join white with sc in any st, sc in each st around, join with sl st in first sc.

***NOTE:** For **double treble crochet (dtr)**, yo 3 times, insert hook in next st, yo, draw lp through, (yo, draw through 2 lps on hook) 4 times.*

continued on next page

Baby's Color Wheel

Continued from page 29

Rnd 11: Ch 7, dtr in same st, *[tr in each of next 2 sts, dc in each of next 2 sts, hdc in each of next 2 sts, sc in each of next 3 sts, hdc in each of next 2 sts, dc in each of next 2 sts, tr in each of next 2 sts], (dtr, ch 2, dtr) in next st; repeat from * 4 more times; repeat between [ ], join with sl st in 5th ch of ch-7 (102 sts, 6 ch sps).

Rnd 12: Ch 3, dc in each st around with (2 dc, ch 2, 2 dc) in each ch sp, join with sl st in top of ch-3, fasten off (21 sts across each side between ch sps.

Holding Hexagons wrong sides together, matching sts, with white, sew together according to Assembly Diagram.

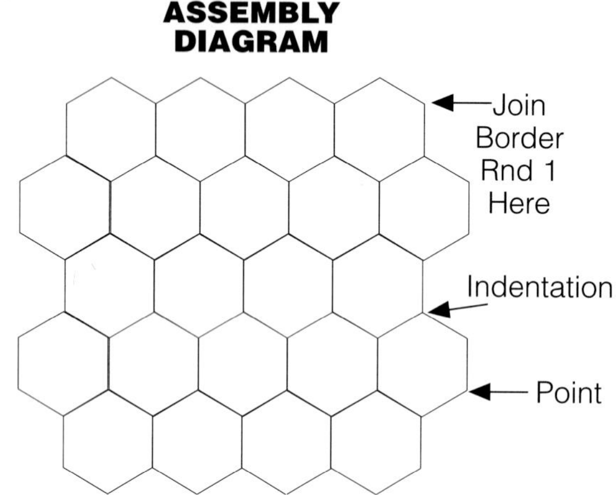

BORDER

***NOTES:** For **sc-decrease (sc-dec),** sc next 2 ch sps or sts tog.*

*For **dc-decrease (dc-dec),** dc next 3 sts tog.*

Rnd 1: Working around entire outer edge, join white with sc in corner ch sp indicated on diagram, sc in each st around with 3 sc in each point and sc-dec in ch sps on each side of seams, join with sl st in first sc, fasten off (788 sc).

Rnd 2: Work this rnd in the following Steps:

Step A: join peach with sl st in **back lp** of center st on first 3-sc group; for **point,** (ch 3, pc, dc) in same st, *pc in **both lps** of next st, (dc in **back lp** of next st, pc in **both lps** of next st) across to center st of next 3-sc group, (dc, pc, dc) in **back lp** of next st, pc in **both lps** of next st, (dc in **back lp** of next st, pc in **both lps** of next st) across to st before next sc-dec, dc-dec in **back lp** of each of next 3 sts*; repeat between ** 2 more times;

Step B: [pc in **both lps** of next st, (dc in **back lp** of next st, pc in **both lps** of next st) across to center st of next 3-sc group, (dc, pc, dc) in **back lp** of next st]; repeat between [ ], pc in **both lps** of next st, (dc in **back lp** of next st, pc in **both lps** of next st) across to st before next sc-dec;

Step C: [dc-dec in **back lp** of each of next 3 sts, *pc in **both lps** of next st, (dc in **back lp** of next st, pc in **both lps** of next st) across to center st of next 3-sc group, (dc, pc, dc) in **back lp** of next st; repeat from *, pc in **both lps** of next st, (dc in **back lp** of next st, pc in **both lps** of next st) across to st before next sc-dec, dc-dec in **back lp** of each of next 3 sts], pc in **both lps** of next st, (dc in **back lp** of next st, pc in **both lps** of next st) across to st before next sc-dec; repeat between [ ], pc in **both lps** of next st, (dc in **back lp** of next st, pc in **both lps** of next st) across to center st of next 3-sc group;

Step D: (dc, pc, dc) in **back lp** of next st; repeat between ** of Step A 3 times;

Step E: repeat Step B.

Step F: repeat Step C, join with sl st in top of ch-3, fasten off.

***NOTE:** For **treble crochet-decrease (tr-dec),** *yo 2 times, insert hook in **front lp** of next st on rnd before last, yo, draw lp through, (yo, draw through 2 lps on hook) 2 times*, skip next st on rnd before last; repeat between **, yo, draw through all 3 lps on hook.*

Rnd 3: Work this rnd in the following Steps:

Step A: join white with sc in first pc, 2 sc in same st; tr in **front lp** of center st of 3-sc group on rnd before last, skip next dc on last rnd behind tr, *sc in next pc on last rnd, (tr in **front lp** of next sc on rnd before last, skip next dc on last rnd behind tr, sc in next pc) across to pc group at next point, tr in **front lp** of center st of next 3-sc group on rnd before last, skip next dc on last rnd behind tr, 3 sc in next pc, tr in **front lp** of same st on rnd before last as last tr, skip next dc on last rnd behind tr, sc in next pc, (tr in **front lp** of next sc on rnd before last, skip next dc on last rnd behind tr, sc in next pc) across to next dc-dec, tr-dec*; repeat between ** 2 more times;

Step B: [sc in next pc on last rnd, (tr in **front lp** of next sc on rnd before last, skip next dc on last rnd behind tr, sc in next pc) across to pc group at next point, tr in **front lp** of center st of next 3-sc group on rnd before last, skip next dc on last rnd behind tr, 3 sc in next pc, tr in **front lp** of same st on rnd before last as last tr, skip next dc on last rnd behind tr]; repeat between [ ], sc in next pc, tr in **front lp** of next sc on rnd before last, skip next dc on last rnd behind tr, sc in next pc) across to next dc-dec;

Step C: [tr-dec, *sc in next pc on last rnd, (tr in **front lp** of next sc on rnd before last, skip next dc on last rnd behind tr, sc in next pc) across to pc-group at next point, tr in **front lp** of center st on next 3 sc group of rnd before last, skip next dc on last rnd behind tr, 3 sc in next pc, tr in **front lp** of same st on rnd before last as last tr, skip next dc on last rnd behind tr; repeat from *, sc in next pc, (tr in **front lp** of next sc on rnd before last, skip next dc on last rnd behind tr, sc in next pc) across to next dc-dec, tr-dec], sc in next pc on last rnd, (tr in **front lp** of next sc on rnd before last, skip next dc on last rnd behind tr, sc in next pc) across to next dc-dec; repeat between [ ], sc in next pc on last rnd, (tr in **front lp** of next sc on rnd before last, skip next dc on last rnd behind tr, sc in next pc) across to pc-group at next point, tr in **front lp** of center st of next 3-dc group on rnd before last, skip next dc on last rnd behind tr;

Step D: 3 sc in next pc, tr in **front lp** of same st on rnd before last as last tr, skip next dc on last rnd behind tr; repeat between ** in Step A 3 times;

Step E: repeat Step B;

Step F: repeat Step C, join with sl st in first sc, fasten off.

Rnd 4: Join variegated with sl st in center st of first 3-sc point, ch 3, 4 dc in same st, dc in each st around with 5 dc in center st of each 3-sc point and dc-dec in 3 sts at each indentation, join with sl st in top of ch-3, fasten off.

***NOTE:** For **sc-decrease (sc-dec) on remainder of pattern,** sc next 3 sts tog.*

Rnd 5: Join white with sc in center st of first 5-dc point, 2 sc in same st, sc in each st around with 3 sc in center st of each 5-dc point and sc-dec at each indentation, join with sl st in first sc, fasten off.

Rnd 6: With lavender, repeat rnd 2.

Rnd 7: With white, repeat rnd 3. At end of rnd, **do not** fasten off.

Rnd 8: Ch 1, sc in first st, 3 sc in next st, sc in each st around with 3 sc in center st of each 3-sc point and sc-dec at each indentation, join.

Rnd 9: Ch 1, sc in first st, skip next st, 6 dc in next st, skip next st, (sc in next st, skip next st, 6 dc in next st, skip next st) around, join, fasten off.◆

Blessed Moments

Instructions on page 26

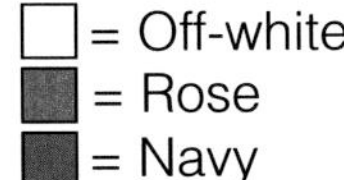

GRAPH

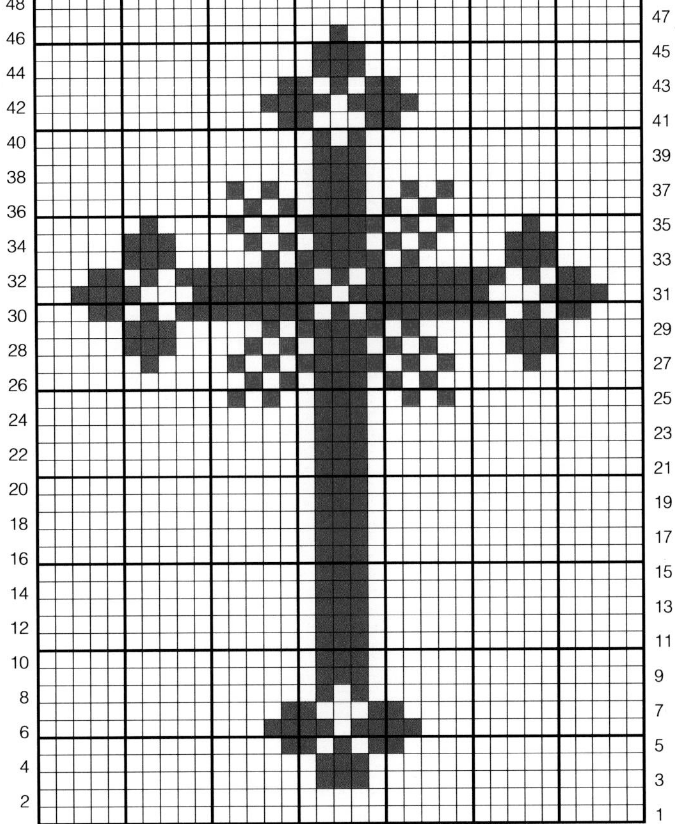

Each square on graph = 1 sc.

Sherbert shades intermingled with textured design stir joyful childhood memories, "The ice cream man is here!"

Ice Cream Cones

by MARGRET WILLSON

SIZE: 45½" x 53½".

MATERIALS: Worsted-weight yarn — 25 oz. gold, 6 oz. each pink, off-white and green; H crochet hook or size needed to obtain gauge.

GAUGE: One 7-dc group and 1 sc = 2"; 3-dc rows = 2".

SKILL LEVEL: ☆☆ Average

Row 1: With gold, ch 189, 3 dc in 9th ch from hook, ch 2, skip next 3 chs, dc in next ch, (ch 2, skip next 3 chs, 3 dc in next ch, ch 2, skip next 3 chs, dc in next ch) across, turn (93 dc, 46 ch sps).

Row 2: Ch 4, skip next ch sp, 2 dc in next st, dc in next st, 2 dc in next st, ch 1, skip next ch sp, dc in next st, (ch 1, skip next ch sp, 2 dc in next st, dc in next st, 2 dc in next st, ch 1, skip next ch sp, dc in next st) across, turn, fasten off (139 dc).

Row 3: For **ice cream,** join pink with sc in first st, (skip next ch sp, skip next 2 sts, 7 dc in next st, skip next 2 sts, skip next ch sp, sc in next st) across, turn, fasten off (24 sc, 23 7-dc groups).

Row 4: Join gold with sl st in first sc, ch 6, sc in center st of next 7-dc group, ch 3, dc in next sc, (ch 3, sc in center st of next 7-dc group, ch 3, dc in next sc) across, turn (47 sts).

Row 5: Ch 3, dc in same st, ch 2, skip next ch sp, dc in next st, (ch 2, skip next ch sp, 3 dc in next st, ch 2, skip next ch sp, dc in next st) across to last ch sp and st, ch 2, skip next ch sp, 2 dc in last st, turn (93 sts).

Row 6: Ch 3, 2 dc in next st, ch 1, skip next ch sp, dc in next st, ch 1, skip next ch sp, (2 dc in next st, dc in next st, 2 dc in next st, ch 1, skip next ch sp, dc in next st, ch 1, skip next ch sp) across to last 2 sts, 2 dc in next st, dc in last st, turn, fasten off (139 dc).

Row 7: For **ice cream,** join off-white with sl st in first st, ch 3, 3 dc in same st, skip next 2 sts, sc in next st, skip next 2 sts, (7 dc in next st, skip next 2 sts, sc in next st, skip next 2 sts) across to last st, 4 dc in last st, turn, fasten off (23 sc, 22 7-dc groups, 8 dc).

Row 8: Join gold with sc in first dc, ch 2, dc in next sc, ch 2, (sc in center st of next 7-dc group, ch 2, dc in next sc, ch 2) across to last 4 dc, skip next 3 dc, sc in last dc, turn.

Row 9: Ch 5, 3 dc in next dc, ch 2, dc in next sc, (ch 2, 3 dc in next dc, ch 2, dc in next sc) across, turn.

Rows 10-100: Working ice cream rows in color sequence of green, pink and off-white, repeat rows 2-9 consecutively, ending with row 4 and pink on last ice cream row.

continued on page 39

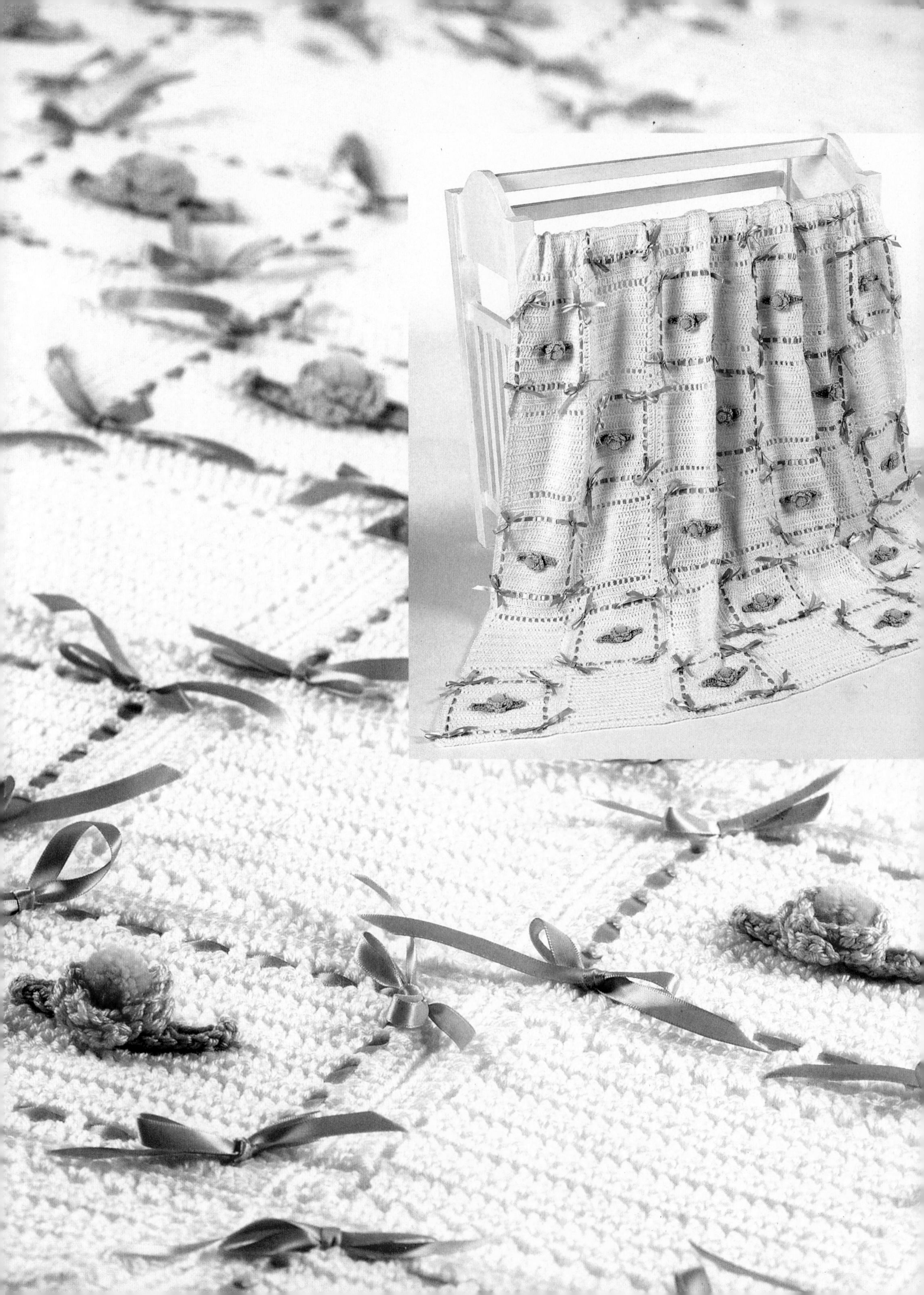

Appealing to the eye as well as the heart, cradle your baby in pure white delicately accented with roses and ribbon trim.

Ribbons and Roses

by SANDRA MILLER MAXFIELD

SIZE: $52\frac{1}{2}$" x $67\frac{1}{2}$".

MATERIALS: Worsted-weight yarn — 35 oz. white, $3\frac{1}{2}$ oz. each green and pink, 2 oz. yellow; 64 yds. purple $\frac{3}{8}$" satin ribbon; white sewing thread; sewing and tapestry needles; G crochet hook or size needed to obtain gauge.

GAUGE: 4 sts = 1"; 2 dc rows = 1". Each Block is $7\frac{1}{2}$" square.

SKILL LEVEL: ☆☆ Average

BLOCK (make 63)

Row 1: With white, ch 30, dc in 6th ch from hook, (ch 1, skip next ch, dc in next ch) across, turn (14 dc, 13 ch sps).

Row 2: Ch 4, skip next ch sp, dc in next st, (dc in next ch sp, dc in next st) 11 times, ch 1, dc in 3rd ch of ch-4, turn (25 dc, 2 ch sps).

Rows 3-12: Ch 4, skip next ch sp, dc in next 23 sts, ch 1, skip next ch sp, dc in last st, turn.

Row 13: Ch 4, skip next ch sp, dc in next st, (ch 1, skip next st, dc in next st) 11 times, ch 1, skip next ch sp, dc in last st, **do not** turn.

Rnd 14: Working around outer edge in ends of rows and in ch sps, ch 3, (2 dc, ch 3, 3 dc) in first row, 2 dc in each row and in each ch sp around with (3 dc, ch 3, 3 dc) in each corner ch sp, join with sl st in top of ch-3, fasten off.

Holding Blocks wrong sides together, matching sts, with white, sew together through **back lps** in 7 rows of 9 Blocks each.

LEAVES (make 32)

With green, (ch 10, sc in 2nd ch from hook, hdc in each of next 2 chs, dc in each of next 2 chs, tr in each of next 2 chs, dc in next ch, sc in last ch) 2 times, fasten off.

ROSE (make 32)

Rnd 1: With pink, ch 4, sl st in first ch to form ring, ch 1, (sc in ring, ch 2) 5 times, join with sl st in first sc (5 ch sps).

Rnd 2: Ch 1, (sc, hdc, dc, hdc, sc) in each ch sp around, join, fasten off (5 petals).

Rnd 3: Working behind petals into beginning ring, join pink with sc in ring between any 2 sts of rnd 1, ch 3, (sc in ring between next 2 sts of rnd 1, ch 3) 4 times, join (5 ch sps).

Rnd 4: Ch 1, (sc, hdc, 2 dc, hdc, sc) in each ch sp around, join, fasten off.

Sew Leaves and Roses centered over every other Block as shown in photo.

For **pom-pom** (make 32), with yellow, wrap yarn around 2 fingers 10 times; slide loops off fin-

continued on page 44

Sending sweet dreams,
gossamer clouds softly float by,
perched on angel wings,
among patches of blue sky.

Spring Breeze

by BRENDA STRATTON
for CROCHET TRENDS & TRADITIONS

SIZE: 52" x 71".

MATERIALS: Worsted-weight yarn — 40 oz. white, 35 oz. blue and 10 oz. yellow; tapestry needle; H crochet hook or size needed to obtain gauge.

GAUGE: Rnds 1-2 = 3" across. Each Hexagon is 8½" across.

SKILL LEVEL: ☆☆ Average

FIRST MOTIF

Rnd 1: With blue, ch 4, sl st in first ch to form ring, ch 4, (dc in ring, ch 1) 5 times, join with sl st in 3rd ch of ch-4 (6 dc, 6 ch sps).

NOTES: *For **beginning tr-cluster (beg tr-cl),** ch 3, *yo 2 times, insert hook in same st or sp, yo, draw lp through, (yo, draw through 2 lps on hook) 2 times; repeat from *, yo, draw through all 3 lps on hook.*

*For **tr-cluster (tr-cl),** yo 2 times, insert hook in next st or chsp, yo, draw lp through, (yo, draw through 2 lps on hook) 2 times, *yo 2 times, insert hook in same st or sp, yo, draw lp through, (yo, draw through 2 lps on hook) 2 times; repeat from *, yo, draw through all 4 lps on hook.*

Rnd 2: Sl st in next ch sp, (beg tr-cl, ch 2, tr-cl) in same sp, ch 2, *(tr-cl, ch 2, tr-cl) in next ch sp, ch 2; repeat from * around, join with sl st in top of first tr-cl, fasten off (12 tr-cls, 12 ch sps).

Rnd 3: Join white with sl st in any ch sp, ch 3, 4 dc in same sp, (*dc in next tr-cl, 2 dc in next ch sp, dc in next tr-cl*, 5 dc in next ch sp) 5 times; repeat between **, join with sl st in top of ch-3 (54 dc).

Rnd 4: Sl st in each of next 2 sts, ch 1, (sc, ch 3, sc) in same st, *[ch 3, skip next 2 sts, (sc in next st, ch 3, skip next 2 sts) 2 times], (sc, ch 3, sc) in next st; repeat from * 4 more times; repeat between [ ], join with sl st in first sc, fasten off (24 ch sps).

Rnd 5: Join yellow with sc in first ch sp, 2 sc in same sp, 3 sc in each ch sp around, join, fasten off (24 3-sc groups).

NOTES: *For **large V-stitch (lg V-st),** (dc, ch 1, dc) in next st.*

*For **beginning shell (beg shell),** ch 3, (dc, ch 2, 2 dc) in same st.*

*For **shell,** (2 dc, ch 2, 2 dc) in next st.*

Rnd 6: Join white with sl st in center st of first 3-sc group, beg shell, *[lg V-st in center st of each of next 3 3-sc groups], shell in center st of next 3-sc group; repeat from * 4 more times; repeat between [ ], join with sl st in top of ch-3 (18 lg V-sts, 6 shells).

Rnd 7: Sl st in next st, sl st in next ch sp, ch 1, (sc, ch 4, sc) in same sp, *[ch 4, sc in ch sp of next

continued on page 38

Spring Breeze

Continued from page 36

lg V-st, ch 4, skip next lg V-st, sc in ch sp of next lg V-st, ch 4], (sc, ch 4, sc) in ch sp of next shell; repeat from * 4 more times; repeat between [ ], join with sl st in first sc, fasten off (24 ch sps).

Rnd 8: Join blue with sl st in first ch sp, ch 2, (3 dc, hdc) in same sp, (hdc, 3 dc, hdc) in each ch sp around, join with sl st in top of ch-2, fasten off (120 sts).

Rnd 9: For **flower,** working in beginning ring between sts of rnd 1, join blue with sl st between any 2 sts, ch 3, (sl st in ring between next 2 sts, ch 3) 5 times, join with sl st in first sl st, fasten off.

With yellow, using French Knot (see illustration), embroider center of flower.

FRENCH KNOT

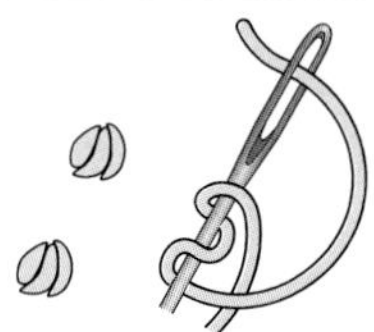

Rnd 10: For **cluster trim,** working around posts of each sc on rnd 4, with blue, join with sl st around post of any st, *[ch 2, (yo, insert hook around post of same st, yo, draw lp through, yo, draw through 2 lps on hook) 2 times, yo, draw through all 3 lps on hook], sl st around post of next st; repeat from * around; repeat between [ ], join with sl st in first sl st, fasten off.

Rnd 11: Working in **back lps,** join white with sl st in first st of rnd 8, sl st in next st, *[(sc, ch 3, sc) in next st, sl st in each of next 2 sts; working over last rnd, sl st in **both lps** of next st on rnd before last]; working in **back lps,** sl st in each of next 2 sts on last rnd; repeat from * around to last 3 sts; repeat between [ ], join, fasten off.

1-SIDE JOINED MOTIF

Rnds 1-10: Repeat same rnds of First Motif.

*NOTE: For **joining ch-3 sp,** ch 1, sl st in corresponding ch sp on other Motif, ch 1.*

Rnd 11: Working in **back lps,** join white with sl st in first st, sl st in next st, joining to side of other Motif (see Joining Diagram), *sc in next st on this Motif, work joining ch-3 sp, sc in same st on this Motif, sl st in each of next 2 sts; working over last rnd, sl st in **both lps** of next st on rnd before last; working in **back lps,** sl st in each of next 2 sts on last rnd; repeat from * 4 more times; [◊(sc, ch 3, sc) in next st, sl st in each of next 2 sts; working over last rnd, sl st in **both lps** of next st on rnd before last◊; working in **back lps,** sl st in each of next 2 sts on last rnd]; repeat between [ ] around to last 3 sts; repeat between ◊◊, join, fasten off.

2-SIDE JOINED MOTIF

Rnds 1-10: Repeat same rnds of First Motif.

Rnd 11: Working in **back lps,** join white with sl st in first st, sl st in next st; joining to other Motif (see diagram), *sc in next st on this Motif, work joining ch-3 sp, sc in same st on this Motif, sl st in each of next 2 sts; working over last rnd, sl st in **both lps** of next st on rnd before last; working in **back lps,** sl st in each of next 2 sts on last rnd*; repeat between ** 4 more times; joining to next Motif, repeat between ** 4 more times, [◊(sc, ch 3, sc) in next st, sl st in each of next 2 sts; working over last rnd, sl st in **both lps of** next st on rnd before last◊; working in **back lps,** sl st in each of next 2 sts on last rnd]; repeat between [ ] around to last 3 sts; repeat between ◊◊, join, fasten off.

3-SIDE JOINED MOTIF

Rnds 1-10: Repeat same rnds of First Motif.

Rnd 11: Working in **back lps,** join white with sl st in first st, sl st in next st; joining to other Motif (see diagram), *sc in next st on this Motif, work joining ch-3 sp, sc in same st on this Motif, sl st in each of next 2 sts; working over last rnd, sl st in **both lps** of next st on rnd before last; working in **back lps,** sl st in each of next 2 sts on last rnd*; repeat between ** 4 more times; joining to next

Motif, repeat between ** 4 more times; joining to next Motif, repeat between ** 4 more times, [◊(sc, ch 3, sc) in next st, sl st in each of next 2 sts; working over last rnd, sl st in **both lps** of next st on rnd before last◊; working in **back lps,** sl st in each of next 2 sts on last rnd]; repeat between [ ] around to last 3 sts; repeat between ◊◊, join, fasten off.

Work and join Motifs according to Joining Diagram.

BORDER

NOTES: *For* ***corner,*** *(2 hdc, ch 2, 2 hdc) in next ch sp.*

For ***beginning corner (beg corner),*** *ch 2, (hdc, ch 2, 2 hdc) in same sp.*

For ***small V-st (sm V-st),*** *(hdc, ch 2, hdc) in next joining or ch sp.*

Work the Border in the following Steps:

Step A: Working around entire outer edge, join white with sl st in corner ch sp before one short end as indicated on diagram, beg corner, *[ch 1, skip next 3 sts, dc in next st, ch 1, (sm V-st in next ch sp, ch 1, skip next 3 sts, dc in next st, ch 1) 3 times, corner in next ch sp, ch 1, skip next 3 sts, dc in next st, ch 1; repeat between ( ) 3 times], sm V-st in next joining; repeat from * 4 more times; repeat between [ ];

Step B: Corner in next corner ch sp, [◊*ch 1, skip next 3 sts, dc in next st, ch 1, (sm V-st in next ch sp, ch 1, skip next 3 sts, dc in next st, ch 1) 3 times*, corner in next ch sp, ch 1, skip next 3 sts, dc in next st, ch 1; repeat between ( ) 3 times◊, sm V-st in next joining; repeat between **, sm V-st in next joining]; repeat between [ ] 3 more times; repeat between ◊◊;

Step C: Corner in next corner ch sp, *[ch 1, skip next 3 sts, dc in next st, ch 1, (sm V-st in next ch sp, ch 1, skip next 3 sts, dc in next st, ch 1) 3 times, corner in next ch sp, ch 1, skip next 3 sts, dc in next st, ch 1; repeat between ( ) 3 times], sm V-st in next joining; repeat from * 4 more times; repeat between [ ];

Step D: Repeat Step B, join with sl st in top of ch-2, fasten off.◆

JOINING DIAGRAM

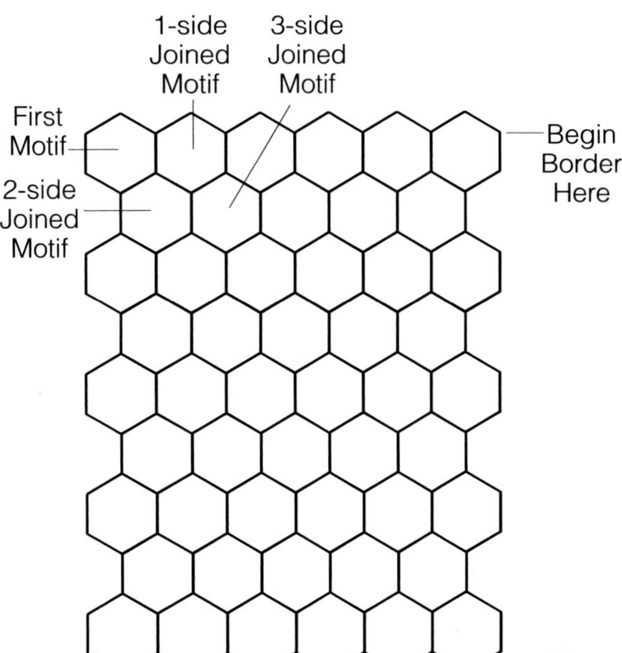

Ice Cream Cones

Continued from page 32

Rnd 101: Sl st in first ch sp, ch 3, (2 dc, ch 3, 3 dc) in same sp, dc in next st, (3 dc in next ch sp, dc in next st) across to last ch sp, (3 dc, ch 3, 3 dc) in last sp leaving last st unworked, dc in end of next row, (3 dc in end of next row, dc in end of next row) across to last row, skip last row; working in starting ch on opposite side of row 1, (3 dc, ch 3, 3 dc) in first ch-3 sp, dc in next ch, (3 dc in next ch-3 sp, dc in next st) across to last ch-3 sp, (3 dc, ch 3, 3 dc) in last ch-3 sp, dc in top of first row, (3 dc in end of next row, dc in end of next row) across to last row, skip last row, join with sl st in top of ch-3 (183 sts across each short end between corner ch sps; 203 sts across each long edge between corner ch sps).

NOTE: *For* ***V-stitch (V-st),*** *(dc, ch 3, dc) in next st or ch sp.*

Rnd 102: Sl st in each of next 2 dc, ch 5, dc in same st, *[V-st in next corner ch sp, V-st in next dc, skip next 2 dc, V-st in next dc, (skip next 3-dc group, V-st in next dc) across] to 3 dc before next corner ch sp, skip next 2 dc, V-st in next dc; repeat from * 2 more times; repeat between [ ], join with sl st in 3rd ch of ch-5.

Rnd 103: Sl st in ch sp of first V-st, ch 3, 3 dc in same sp, 4 dc in ch sp of each V-st around with 9 tr in ch sp of each corner V-st, join with sl st in top of ch-3, fasten off.◆

Blends of simple stitches and fresh color co-mingle to create a vintage one-piece classic loved ones will treasure.

Grape Vineyard

by TAMMY HILDEBRAND

SIZE: 39" x 60½".

MATERIALS: Worsted-weight yarn — 9 oz. green, 8 oz. each lt. and dk. purple; I crochet hook or size needed to obtain gauge.

GAUGE: Four 3-dc groups and 4 sc = 5"; 7 pattern rows = 4".

SKILL LEVEL: ☆☆ Average

Row 1: With dk. purple, ch 122, sc in 2nd ch from hook, (skip next ch, 3 dc in next ch, skip next ch, sc in next ch) across, **do not** turn, fasten off (31 sc, 30 3-dc groups).

***NOTE:** For **V-stitch (V-st)**, (dc, ch 2, dc) in next st.*

Row 2: Join green with sl st in first sc, ch 4, skip next 3-dc group, (V-st in next sc, ch 1, skip next 3-dc group) across to last sc, dc in last sc, **do not** turn, fasten off (30 ch-1 sps, 29 V-sts, 2 dc).

Row 3: Join lt. purple, with sc in 3rd ch of ch-4, sc in next ch, (3 dc in ch sp of next V-st, sc in next ch-1 sp) across to last dc, sc in last dc, **do not** turn, fasten off (32 sc, 29 3-dc groups).

Row 4: Join green with sl st in first st, ch 4, V-st in next sc, (ch 1, skip next 3-dc group, V-st in next sc) across to last sc, ch 1, dc in last sc, **do not** turn, fasten off.

Row 5: Join dk. purple, with sc in 3rd ch of ch-4, 3 dc in next V-st, (sc in next ch-1 sp, 3 dc in next V-st) across to last dc, sc in last dc, **do not** turn, fasten off.

Rows 6-101: Repeat rows 2-5 consecutively. At end of last row, **do not** turn or fasten off.

EDGING

Row 1: For **first side,** working in ends of rows, ch 1, sc in each sc row and 3 dc in each dc row across to last row, (sc, ch 1, sl st) in last row, fasten off.

Row 2: For **2nd side,** working in ends of rows on opposite side, join dk. purple with sl st in end of first row, ch 1, sc in same row, 3 dc in each dc row and sc in each sc row across to last row, (sc, ch 1, sl st) in last row, fasten off.◆

Quick and easy, this playful mile-a-minute® design, sends sweet treats of a warm, cozy and more lasting kind.

Lollipops

by DIANA SIPPEL
of DIANA LYNN'S DESIGNS

SIZE: 30" x 38".

MATERIALS: Baby yarn — 7 oz. white, $1\frac{3}{4}$ oz. each pink, green, yellow, blue and purple; F crochet hook or size needed to obtain gauge.

GAUGE: Each Lollipop is $1\frac{3}{4}$" across. Each Strip is $3\frac{1}{2}$" wide.

SKILL LEVEL: ☆☆ Average

STRIP (make 8)

First Lollipop

Rnd 1: With pink, ch 4, sl st in first ch to form ring, ch 3, 15 dc in ring, join with sl st in top of ch-3 (16 dc).

Rnd 2: Ch 10, sl st in same st, ch 2, (sl st in next st, ch 2) around, join with sl st in joining sl st of last rnd, fasten off.

Next Lollipop

Rnd 1: With green, ch 4, drop lp from hook, insert hook in ch-10 lp of last Lollipop made, draw dropped lp through, sl st in first ch to form ring, ch 3, 15 dc in ring, join with sl st in top of ch-3 (16 dc).

Rnd 2: Ch 10, sl st in same st, ch 2, (sl st in next st, ch 2) around, join with sl st in joining sl st of last rnd, fasten off.

Working in color sequence of yellow, blue, purple, pink and green, repeat Next Lollipop 18 more times ending with purple.

Last Lollipop

Rnd 1: With pink, ch 4, drop lp from hook, insert hook in ch-10 lp of last Lollipop made, draw dropped lp through, sl st in first ch to form ring, ch 3, 15 dc in ring, join with sl st in top of ch-3 (16 dc).

Rnd 2: Ch 2, (sl st in next st, ch 2) around, join with sl st in joining sl st of last rnd, fasten off.

Edging

Rnd 1: Working around outer edge of Strip, join white with sl st in any ch sp on Last Lollipop, ch 3, *(sc in next ch sp, ch 1) 9 times, hdc in next ch sp, ch 1, dc next ch sp and 2nd ch sp on next Lollipop tog, ch 1, (hdc in next ch sp, ch 1, sc in next ch sp, ch 1, hdc in next ch sp, ch 1, dc next ch sp and 2nd ch sp on next Lollipop tog, ch 1) 19 times*, hdc in next ch sp, ch 1; repeat between **, join with sl st in 2nd ch of ch-3 (176 ch sps).

Rnd 2: Sl st in next ch sp, ch 1, 2 sc in same sp, 3 sc in each of next 8 ch sps, 2 sc in each of next 80 ch sps, 3 sc in each of next 8 ch sps, 2 sc in each of next 79 ch sps, join with sl st in first sc (368 sc).

Rnd 3: Working this rnd in **back lps** only, ch 1,

continued on next page

Lollipops

Continued from page 43

sc in each st around, join.

Rnd 4: Ch 1, sc in first st, ch 1, skip next st, (sc in next st, ch 1, skip next st) around, join.

To **join Strips,** holding 2 Strips side by side with right sides facing you, with white, leaving 10 ch sps at each end of Strips unworked, join white with sl st in first ch sp on this Strip, ch 2, sl st in first ch sp on other Strip, (ch 2, sl st in next ch sp on this Strip, ch 2, sl st in next ch sp on other Strip) across, fasten off.

Join remaining Strips in same manner.

BORDER

Working around entire outer edge, join white with sl st in any ch sp, ch 3, (sl st in next ch sp, ch 3) around, join with sl st in first sl st, fasten off.◆

Ribbons and Posies

Continued from page 35

gers. Tie separate strand yellow tightly around center of all loops; cut loops at each end. Trim pom-pom to ¾". Sew one pom-pom to center of each rose.

FINISHING

Cut 4 pieces ribbon each 18" long; beginning and ending in corners, weave piece through ch sps across one edge of one flower Block. Repeat with remaining pieces across each edge; tie ends into a bow at corners. Repeat on remaining flower Blocks.

Tack bows to Afghan to secure.◆

Mothers, Friends & Gardens

Chapter Three

Delightful Daffodils
Grandmother's Flowers
Floral Hexagon
Flower Garden
Floral Bounty
Pansies
Midsummer Nights

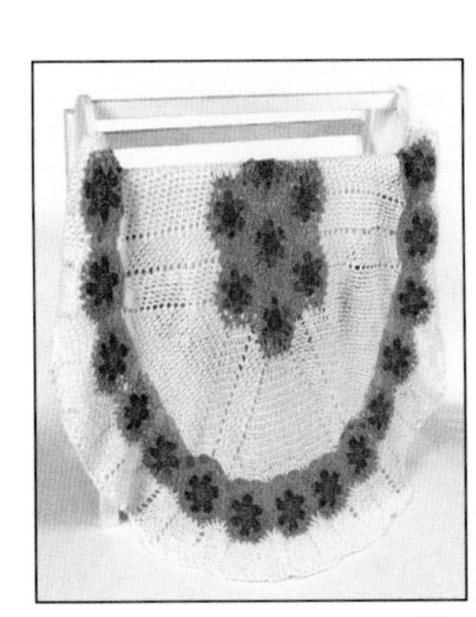

Afghan Splendor

A lovely spring display dancing in the winds, drifts artistically across this yarn canvas in a collage of colorful blends.

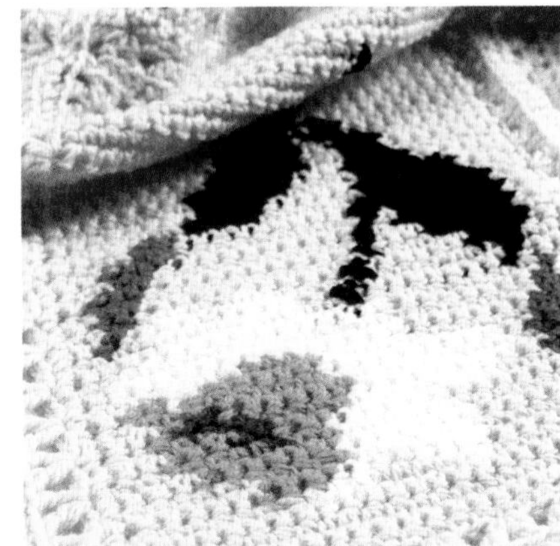

Delightful Daffodils

by MAGGIE WELDON

SIZE: 44½" x 68½".

MATERIALS: Worsted-weight yarn — 39 oz. yellow, 4 oz. each dk. teal, lt. teal, gold, brown and white; tapestry needle; I crochet hook or size needed to obtain gauge.

GAUGE: 3 sc = 1"; 11 sc rows = 3".

SKILL LEVEL: ☆☆ Average

BLOCK (make 16)

Row 1: With yellow, ch 27, sc in 2nd ch from hook, sc in each ch across, turn (26 sc).

Rows 2-4: Ch 1, sc in each st across, turn.

*NOTES: When changing colors (see page 159), always drop yarn to wrong side of work. Use a separate ball or skein of yarn for each color section. **Do not** carry dropped color across from one section to another. Fasten off colors at end of each color section.*

Work odd-numbered graph rows from right to left; work even-numbered rows from left to right.

Each square on graph equals one sc.

Row 5: For **row 5 of graph,** ch 1, sc in first 15 sts changing to dk. teal in last st made, sc in next st changing to yellow, sc in last 10 sts, turn.

Rows 6-52: Ch 1, sc in each st across changing colors according to graph on page 55, turn.

Rnd 53: Working in rnds, ch 1, 2 sc in first st, sc in each st across to last st, 3 sc in last st; *working in ends of rows, skip first 2 rows, sc in each row across to last 2 rows, skip last 2 rows*; working in starting ch on opposite side of row 1, 3 sc in first ch, sc in each ch across with 3 sc in last ch; repeat between **, sc in same st as first sc, join with sl st in first sc (26 sc across each short end between center corner sts, 50 sc across each long edge between center corner sts).

*NOTES: For **beginning V-stitch (beg V-st),** ch 4, dc in same st.*

*For **V-stitch (V-st),** (dc, ch 1, dc) in next st.*

Rnd 54: Beg V-st, ch 2, V-st in same st, skip next 2 sts, (V-st in next st, skip next 2 sts) across to next center corner st, *(V-st, ch 2, V-st) in next st, skip next 2 sts, (V-st in next st, skip next 2 sts) across to next center corner st; repeat from * around, join with sl st in 3rd ch of ch-4, fasten off.

Holding Blocks wrong sides together, matching sts, with yellow, sew together through **back lps** in 4 rows of 4 Blocks each.

BORDER

*NOTE: For **picot,** ch 4, sl st in 4th ch from hook.*

Working around entire outer edge, join yellow with sl st in any corner ch sp, ch 7, sl st in 4th ch

continued on page 55

Petite, white blossoms flutter delightfully in their colorful alternating parade of traditional-style granny squares.

Grandmother's Flowers

by MAGGIE WELDON

SIZE: 45" x 61".

MATERIALS: Worsted-weight yarn — 21 oz. white, 14 oz. blue and 11 oz. pink; tapestry needle; I crochet hook or size needed to obtain gauge.

GAUGE: Each Square is 4" square.

SKILL LEVEL: ☆☆ Average

SQUARE (make 83 white, 42 pink and 40 blue)

Rnd 1: Ch 4, sl st in first ch to form ring, ch 3, 2 dc in ring, ch 3, (3 dc in ring, ch 3) 3 times, join with sl st in top of ch-3 (12 dc, 4 ch sps).

Rnd 2: Ch 3, dc in each of next 2 sts, (2 dc, ch 3, 2 dc) in next ch sp, *dc in each of next 3 sts, (2 dc, ch 3, 2 dc) in next ch sp; repeat from * around, join (28 dc, 4 ch sps).

Rnd 3: Ch 3, dc in next 4 sts, (2 dc, ch 3, 2 dc) in next ch sp, *dc in next 7 sts, (2 dc, ch 3, 2 dc) in next ch sp; repeat from * around to last 2 sts, dc in each of last 2 sts, join, fasten off (44 dc, 4 ch sps).

Holding Squares wrong sides together, matching sts, with white, sew together through **back lps** according to Assembly Diagram.

ASSEMBLY DIAGRAM

FLOWER (make 82)

With white, ch 4, sl st in first ch to form ring, (ch 2, dc, ch 2, sl st) 5 times in ring, fasten off.

To secure Flowers to pink and blue Squares; working through both thicknesses of Flower and Square, embroider 3 blue French Knots (see illustration) over Flower and each pink Square; embroider 3 pink French Knots over Flower and each blue Square.

FRENCH KNOT

BORDER

Working around entire outer edge of Squares, join blue with sl st in any corner ch sp, ch 3, (dc, ch 2, 2 dc) in same sp, dc in each st around with dc ch sps on each side of seams tog and (2 dc, ch 2, 2 dc) in each corner ch sp, join with sl st in top of ch-3, fasten off.◆

Beautiful colors and joining illustrations combine to bring you a glorious coverlet that's also a pleasure to stitch.

Floral Hexagon

SIZE: 53½" across.

MATERIALS: Worsted-weight yarn — 12 oz. off-white, 6 oz. each lt. rose, dk. rose and green; J crochet hook or size needed to obtain gauge.

GAUGE: Rnds 1-3 of Motif = 3½" across; 3 dc = 1"; 3 dc rows = 2". Each Motif is 5" across.

SKILL LEVEL: ☆☆☆ Advanced

CENTER MOTIFS

Motif No. 1

Rnd 1: With dk. rose, ch 4, sl st in first ch to form ring, ch 1, (sc in ring, tr in ring) 6 times, join with sl st in first sc (6 tr, 6 sc).

Rnd 2: Ch 3, skip next st, (sl st in next st, ch 3, skip next st) around, join with sl st in joining sl st of last rnd, fasten off (6 ch sps).

Rnd 3: For **petals,** join lt. rose with sl st in any ch sp, ch 3, (dc, tr, 2 dc, sl st) in same sp, ch 2, *(sl st, ch 3, dc, tr, 2 dc, sl st) in next ch sp, ch 2; repeat from * around, join with sl st in first sl st, fasten off (6 petals, 6 ch sps).

Rnd 4: Join green with sl st in any ch sp, ch 5, dc in same sp, ch 2, sc in **front lp** of tr in center of next petal, ch 2, *(dc, ch 2, dc) in next ch sp, ch 2, sc in **front lp** of tr in center of next petal, ch 2; repeat from * around, join with sl st in 3rd ch of ch-5 (18 ch sps).

Rnd 5: Sl st in first ch sp, ch 5, hdc in same sp, ch 2, sc in next ch sp, ch 3, sc in next ch sp, ch 2, *(hdc, ch 3, hdc) in next ch sp, ch 2, sc in next ch sp, ch 3, sc in next ch sp, ch 2; repeat from * around, join with sl st in 2nd ch of ch-5, fasten off (12 ch-3 sps, 12 ch-2 sps).

Motif No. 2

Rnds 1-4: Repeat same rnds of Motif No. 1.

Rnd 5: Sl st in first ch sp; joining to previous Motif (see Joining Diagram I), ch 4, sl st in ch-3 sp between any 2 hdc, ch 2, hdc in same sp on this

JOINING DIAGRAM I

I = Joining

continued on next page

Floral Hexagon

Continued from page 51

Motif, ch 2, sc in next ch sp, ch 2, sl st in next ch-3 sp on other Motif, ch 2, sc in next ch sp on this Motif, ch 2, hdc in next ch sp, ch 2, sl st in next ch-3 sp on other Motif, ch 2, hdc in same sp on this Motif, ch 2, sc in next ch sp, ch 3, sc in next ch sp, ch 2, *(hdc, ch 3, hdc) in next ch sp, ch 2, sc in next ch sp, ch 3, sc in next ch sp, ch 2; repeat from * around, join with sl st in 2nd ch of ch-4, fasten off.

Motif Nos. 3-6

Rnds 1-4: Repeat same rnds of Motif No. 1 on page 51.

Rnd 5: Sl st in first ch sp; joining to previous Motif (see Joining Diagram I on page 51), ch 4, sl st in corresponding ch-3 sp between 2 hdc, ch 2, hdc in same sp on this Motif, ch 2, sc in next ch sp, *ch 2, sl st in next ch-3 sp on other Motif, ch 2, sc in next ch sp on this Motif, ch 2, hdc in next ch sp, ch 2, sl st in next ch-3 sp on other Motif, ch 2, hdc in same sp on this Motif, ch 2, sc in next ch sp*; joining to Motif No. 1; repeat between **, ch 3, sc in next ch sp, ch 2, [(hdc, ch 3, hdc) in next ch sp, ch 2, sc in next ch sp, ch 3, sc in next ch sp, ch 2]; repeat between [ ] around, join with sl st in 2nd ch of ch-4, fasten off.

Motif No. 7

Rnds 1-4: Repeat same rnds of Motif No. 1.

Rnd 5: Sl st in first ch sp; joining to previous Motif according to Joining Diagram I, ch 4, sl st in corresponding ch-3 sp between 2 hdc, ch 2, hdc in same sp on this Motif, ch 2, sc in next ch sp, *ch 2, sl st in next ch-3 sp on other Motif, ch 2, sc in next ch sp on this Motif, ch 2, hdc in next ch sp, ch 2, sl st in next ch-3 sp on other Motif, ch 2, hdc in same sp on this Motif, ch 2, sc in next ch sp*; joining to Motif No. 1; repeat between **; joining to Motif No. 2; repeat between **, ch 3, sc in next ch sp, ch 2, [(hdc, ch 3, hdc) in next ch sp, ch 2, sc in next ch sp, ch 3, sc in next ch sp, ch 2]; repeat between [ ], join with sl st in 2nd ch of ch-4, fasten off.

AFGHAN

Rnd 1: Working around outer edge of Motif Center, join off-white with sl st in first unworked ch-3 sp after any joining, ch 3, dc in same sp, 2 dc in each of next 2 ch sps, [◊*(dc, ch 2, dc) in next ch sp, 2 dc in each of next 3 ch sps; repeat from *, skip next joining◊, 2 dc in each of next 3 ch sps]; repeat between [ ] 4 more times; repeat between ◊◊, join with sl st in top of ch-3 (132 dc, 12 ch sps).

Rnd 2: Sl st in next st, ch 3, dc in next 5 sts, *[(dc, ch 2, dc) in next ch sp, dc in next 8 sts, (dc, ch 2, dc) in next ch sp, dc in next 6 sts, skip next 2 sts], dc in next 6 sts; repeat from * 4 more times; repeat between [ ], join (144 dc, 12 ch sps).

Rnds 3-14: Sl st in next st, ch 3, dc in next 5 sts *[(dc, ch 2, dc) in next ch sp, dc in each st across to next ch sp, (dc, ch 2, dc) in next ch sp, dc in next 6 sts, skip next 2 sts], dc in next 6 sts; repeat from * 4 more times; repeat between [ ], join, ending with 288 dc and 12 ch sps in last row. At end of last row, fasten off.

OUTER MOTIFS

Motif No. 1

Rnds 1-4: Reversing dk. rose and lt. rose, repeat same rnds of Center Motif No. 1.

Rnd 5: Sl st in first ch sp; joining to last rnd of Afghan, ch 4, sl st in ch sp before any indentation (see Joining Diagram II), ch 2, hdc in same sp on this Motif, ch 2, sc in next ch sp, ch 2, skip next 7 sts on Afghan, sl st in next sp between sts, ch 2, sc in next ch sp on this Motif, ch 2, hdc in next ch sp, ch 2, skip next 7 sts on Afghan, sl st in next ch sp, ch 2, hdc in same sp on this Motif, ch 2, sc in next ch sp, ch 3, sc in next ch sp, ch 2, *(hdc, ch 3, hdc) in next ch sp, ch 2, sc in next ch sp, ch 3, sc in next ch sp, ch 2; repeat from * around, join with sl st in 2nd ch of ch-4, fasten off.

Motif Nos. 2 & 3

Rnds 1-4: Repeat same rnds of Center Motif No. 1, reversing dk. rose and lt. rose.

Rnd 5: Work this rnd in the following steps:

Step A: sl st in first ch sp; joining to previous Motif, ch 4, sl st in corresponding ch-3 sp between 2 hdc (see Joining Diagram II), ch 2, hdc in same sp on this Motif, ch 2, sc in next ch sp, ch 2, sl st in next ch-3 sp on other Motif, ch 2, sc in next ch sp on this Motif, ch 2, hdc in next ch sp;

Step B: joining to last rnd of Afghan, ch 2, sl st in next st on Afghan, ch 2, hdc in same sp on this Motif, ch 2, sc in next ch sp, ch 2, skip next 4 sts on Afghan, sl st in next st, ch 2, sc in next ch sp on this Motif, ch 2, hdc in next ch sp, ch 2, skip next 4 sts, sl st in next st, ch 2, hdc in same sp on this Motif;

Step C: ch 2, sc in next ch sp, ch 3, sc in next ch sp, ch 2, *(hdc, ch 3, hdc) in next ch sp, ch 2, sc in next ch sp, ch 3, sc in next ch sp, ch 2; repeat from * around, join with sl st in 2nd ch of ch-4, fasten off.

JOINING DIAGRAM II

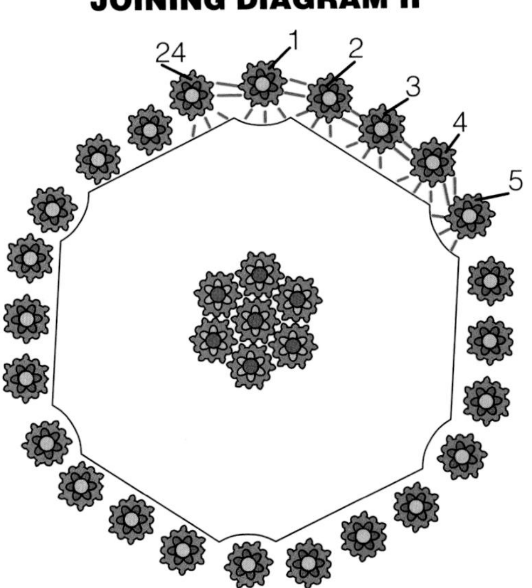

Motif No. 4

Rnds 1-4: Repeat same rnds of Center Motif No. 1, reversing dk. rose and lt. rose.

Rnd 5: Work this rnd in the following steps:

Step A: sl st in first ch sp; joining to previous Motif, ch 4, sl st in corresponding ch-3 sp between 2 hdc (see Joining Diagram II), ch 2, hdc in same sp on this Motif, ch 2, sc in next ch sp, ch 2, sl st in next ch-3 sp on other Motif, ch 2, sc in next ch sp on this Motif, ch 2, hdc in next ch sp;

Step B: joining to last rnd of Afghan, ch 2, sl st in next st on Afghan, ch 2, hdc in same sp on this Motif, ch 2, sc in next ch sp, ch 2, skip next 4 sts on Afghan, sl st in next st, ch 2, sc in next ch sp on this Motif, ch 2, hdc in next ch sp, ch 2, skip next 5 sts, sl st in next st, ch 2, hdc in same sp on this Motif;

Step C: ch 2, sc in next ch sp, ch 3, sc in next ch sp, ch 2, *(hdc, ch 3, hdc) in next ch sp, ch 2, sc in next ch sp, ch 3, sc in next ch sp, ch 2; repeat from * around, join with sl st in 2nd ch of ch-4, fasten off.

Motif No. 5

Working this rnd in the following steps:

Rnds 1-4: Repeat same rnds of Center Motif No. 1, reversing dk. rose and lt. rose.

Rnd 5: Work this rnd in the following steps:

Step A: sl st in first ch sp; joining to previous Motif, ch 4, sl st in corresponding ch-3 sp between 2 hdc (see Joining Diagram II), ch 2, hdc in same sp on this Motif, ch 2, sc in next ch sp, ch 2, sl st in next ch-3 sp on other Motif, ch 2, sc in next ch sp on this Motif, ch 2, hdc in next ch sp;

Step B: joining to last rnd of Afghan, ch 2, sl st in next ch sp (see Joining Diagram II), ch 2, hdc in same sp on this Motif, ch 2, sc in next ch sp, ch 2, skip next 7 sts on Afghan, sl st in next sp between sts, ch 2, sc in next ch sp on this Motif, ch 2, hdc in next ch sp, ch 2, skip next 7 sts on Afghan, sl st in next ch sp, ch 2, hdc in same sp on this Motif;

Step C: ch 2, sc in next ch sp, ch 3, sc in next ch sp, ch 2, *(hdc, ch 3, hdc) in next ch sp, ch 2, sc in next ch sp, ch 3, sc in next ch sp, ch 2; repeat from * around, join with sl st in 2nd ch of ch-4, fasten off.

For **Motif Nos. 6-23,** repeat Motif Nos. 2-5 consecutively, ending with Motif No. 3.

continued on next page

Floral Hexagon

Continued from page 53

Motif No. 24

Rnds 1-4: Repeat same rnds of Center Motif No. 1 on page 51, reversing dk. rose and lt. rose.

Rnd 5: Work this rnd in the following steps: **Step A:** sl st in first ch sp; joining to previous Motif, ch 4, sl st in corresponding ch-3 sp between 2 hdc (see Joining Diagram II on page 53), ch 2, hdc in same sp on this Motif, ch 2, sc in next ch sp, ch 2, sl st in next ch-3 sp on other Motif, ch 2, sc in next ch sp on this Motif, ch 2, hdc in next ch sp;

Step B: joining to last rnd of Afghan, ch 2, sl st in next st on Afghan, ch 2, hdc in same sp on this Motif, ch 2, sc in next ch sp, ch 2, skip next 4 sts on Afghan, sl st in next st, ch 2, sc in next ch sp on this Motif, ch 2, hdc in next ch sp, ch 2, skip next 5 sts on Afghan, sl st in next st, ch 2, hdc in same sp on this Motif, ch 2, sc in next ch sp;

Step C: joining to Motif No. 1, ch 2, sl st in next ch-3 sp on other Motif, ch 2, sc in next ch sp on this Motif, ch 2, hdc in next ch sp, ch 2, sl st in next ch-3 sp on other Motif, ch 2, hdc in same sp on this Motif;

Step D: ch 2, sc in next ch sp, ch 3, sc in next ch sp, ch 2, *(hdc, ch 3, hdc) in next ch sp, ch 2, sc in next ch sp, ch 3, sc in next ch sp, ch 2; repeat from *, join with sl st in 2nd ch of ch-4, fasten off.

REMAINDER OF AFGHAN

Rnd 15: Working around outer edge of Outer Motifs, join off-white with sl st in first unworked ch-3 sp between hdc after any joining, ch 3, 2 dc in each of next 3 ch sps, (dc, ch 2, dc) in next ch sp, dc in each of next 3 ch sps, skip next 2 joining ch sps, dc in each of next 3 ch sps, *(dc, ch 2, dc) in next ch sp, 2 dc in each of next 3 ch sps, (dc, ch 2, dc) in next ch sp, dc in each of next 3 ch sps, skip next 2 joining ch sps, dc in each of next 3 ch sps; repeat from * around, dc in same sp as first st, ch 2, join with sl st in top of ch-3 (384 dc, 48 ch sps).

Rnds 16-20: Ch 3, dc in next 7 sts, ch 2, skip next ch sp, (dc in next 8 sts, ch 2, skip next ch sp) around, join.

Rnd 21: Ch 1, sc in first st, ch 3, skip next st, (sc in next st, ch 3, skip next st) 3 times, sc in next ch sp, ch 3, *(sc in next st, ch 3, skip next st) 4 times, sc in next ch sp, ch 3; repeat from * around, join with sl st in first sc.

Rnd 22: Sl st in first ch sp, ch 1, sc in same sp, ch 3, (sc in next ch sp, ch 3) around, join.

Rnd 23: Sl st in first ch sp, ch 1, 3 sc in same sp, 3 sc in each ch sp around, join, fasten off.◆

Delightful Daffodils

Continued from page 47

from hook, ch 1, dc in same sp, (picot, ch 1, dc) 2 times in same sp, (dc, picot, dc) in each ch sp around to next corner ch sp, *dc in next ch sp, (picot, ch 1, dc) 3 times in same sp, (dc, picot, dc) in each ch sp around to next corner ch sp; repeat from * around, join with sl st in 3rd ch of ch-7, fasten off.◆

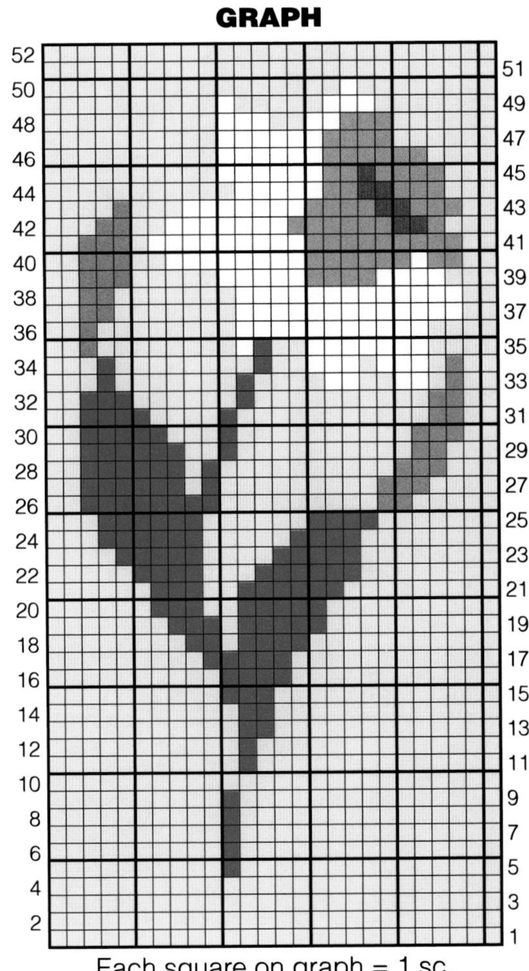

Each square on graph = 1 sc.

Fragrant petals open wide,
standing straight and tall,
whispering in the meadows while
answering summer's call.

Flower Garden

by MAGGIE WELDON

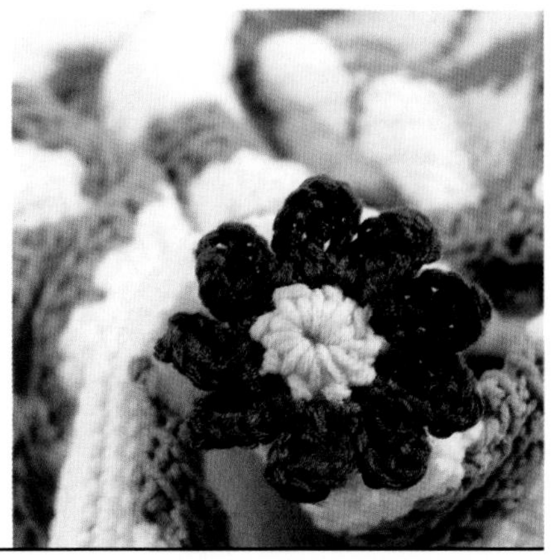

SIZE: 50" x 66".

MATERIALS: Worsted-weight yarn — 40 oz. white, 16 oz. green, 3 oz. purple and 2 oz. yellow; tapestry needle; I crochet hook or size needed to obtain gauge.

GAUGE: 3 sc = 1"; 7 sc rows = 2". Each Block is 7" x 13".

SKILL LEVEL: ☆☆ Average

BLOCK (make 35)

Row 1: With white, ch 18, sc in 2nd ch from hook, sc in each ch across, turn (17 sc).

Row 2: Ch 1, sc in each st across, turn.

NOTES: *When changing colors (see page 159), always drop yarn to wrong side of work. Use a separate skein or ball of yarn for each color section.* ***Do not*** *carry yarn across from one section to another. Fasten off colors at end of each color section.*

Work odd-numbered graph rows from right to left; work even-numbered rows from left to right. Each square on graph equals one sc.

Row 3: Ch 1, sc in first 8 sts changing to green in last st made, sc in next st changing to white, sc in last 8 sts, turn.

Rows 4-39: Ch 1, sc in each st across changing colors according to graph on page 63, turn.

Rnd 40: Working in rnds, ch 1, 3 sc in first st, sc in each st across with 3 sc in last st, evenly space 33 sc across ends of rows; working in starting ch on opposite side of row 1, 3 sc in first ch, sc in each st across with 3 sc in last ch, evenly space 33 sc across ends of rows, join with sl st in first sc, fasten off (17 sc across each short end between corner sc, 35 sc across each long edge between corner sc).

NOTES: *For* ***beginning V-stitch (beg V-st),*** *ch 4, dc in same st.*

For ***V-stitch (V-st),*** *(dc, ch 1, dc) in next st.*

Rnd 41: Join green with sl st in any center corner st, beg V-st, ch 2, V-st in same st, skip next 2 sts, (V-st in next st, skip next 2 sts) across to next center corner st, *(V-st, ch 2, V-st) in next st, ch 2, skip next 2 sts, (V-st in next st, skip next 2 sts) across to next center corner st; repeat from * around, join with sl st in 3rd ch of ch-4, fasten off.

Holding Blocks wrong sides together, matching sts, with green, sew together through **back lps** in 7 rows of 5 Blocks each.

FLOWER (make 35)

Rnd 1: With yellow, ch 3, sl st in first ch to form ring, ch 2, 8 hdc in ring, join with sl st in top of ch-2, fasten off (9 hdc).

continued on page 63

Enhance your indoor
garden with no feeding or mess,
with year 'round
blooms of spectacular finesse.

Floral Bounty

by MAGGIE WELDON

SIZE: 42" x 71".

MATERIALS: Worsted-weight yarn — 23 oz. white, 4 oz. each blue, peach, pink, purple and yellow; tapestry needle; I crochet hook or size needed to obtain gauge.

GAUGE: Rnds 1-4 of Hexagon = 5¾" across. Each Hexagon is 7" across.

SKILL LEVEL: ☆☆ Average

HEXAGON (make 67, see Note)

NOTE: Make 17 each using blue, peach and pink on rnd 3; make 16 using purple on rnd 3.

Rnd 1: With yellow, ch 3, 8 hdc in 3rd ch from hook, join with sl st in top of ch-2 (9 hdc).

Rnd 2: Ch 2, hdc in same st, 2 hdc in each st around, join, fasten off (18).

Rnd 3: Join color (see Note) with sl st in any st, ch 3, (2 dc, ch 2, 3 dc) in same st, skip next 2 sts, *(3 dc, ch 2, 3 dc) in next st, skip next 2 sts; repeat from * around, join with sl st in top of ch-3 (36 dc, 6 ch sps).

Rnd 4: Sl st in each of next 2 sts, sl st in next ch sp, ch 3, (2 dc, ch 3, 3 dc) in same sp, sc in sp between next two 3-dc groups, *(3 dc, ch 3, 3 dc) in next ch sp, sc in sp between next two 3-dc groups; repeat from * around, join, fasten off.

*NOTE: For **half treble crochet (htr)**, yo 2 times, insert hook in next st, yo, draw lp through, yo, draw through 2 lps on hook, yo, draw through all 3 lps on hook.*

Rnd 5: Join white with sc in any ch sp, 2 sc in same sp, ch 2, (htr, ch 2, htr) in next sc, ch 2, *3 sc in next ch sp, ch 2, (htr, ch 2, htr) in next sc, ch 2; repeat from * around, join with sl st in first sc (18 sc, 18 ch sps, 12 htr).

Rnd 6: Ch 3, *[(dc, ch 2, dc) in next st, dc in next st, 2 dc in next ch sp, 3 dc in next ch sp, 2 dc in next ch sp], dc in next st; repeat from * 4 more times; repeat between [ ], join with sl st in top of ch-3, fasten off (11 dc across each side between ch sps).

Holding Hexagons wrong sides together, matching sts, with white, sew together through **back lps** according to Assembly Diagram on page 68.

BORDER

*NOTE: For **decrease (dec)**, sc next 2 ch sps tog skipping seam in between.*

Working around outer edge, join white with sc in ch sp indicated on diagram, ch 6, (sc, ch 5) in same sp, skip next 2 sts, (sc in next st, ch 5, skip next 2 sts) around with (sc, ch 6, sc, ch 5, skip next 2 sts) in each ch sp and (dec, ch 5, skip next

continued on page 68

A soft, lattice-look background warmly welcomes relaxation with graceful displays of textured floral pageantry.

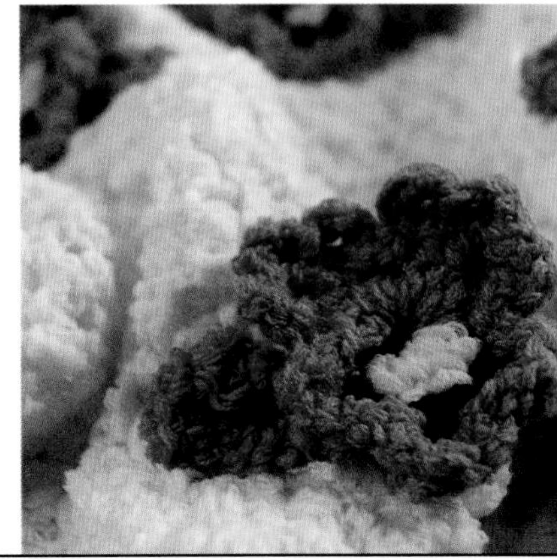

Pansies

by MAGGIE WELDON

SIZE: 42" x 55".

MATERIALS: Terry worsted-weight yarn — 840 yds. ivory, 160 yds. green, 120 yds. lavender and small amount yellow; 3-ply worsted-weight yarn — small amount black; tapestry needle; K and P crochet hooks or sizes needed to obtain gauges.

GAUGES: With **K hook,** Pansy is 4" across. With **P hook,** 6 sc and 5 ch-1 sps = 6"; 5 sc rows worked in pattern = 3".

SKILL LEVEL: ☆☆ Average

AFGHAN

Row 1: With P hook and ivory, ch 80, sc in 2nd ch from hook, (ch 1, skip next ch, sc in next ch) across, turn (40 sc, 39 ch sps).

Row 2: Ch 1, sc in first st, sc in next ch sp, (ch 1, skip next st, sc in next ch sp) across to last st, sc in last st, turn (41 sc, 38 ch sps).

Row 3: Ch 1, sc in first st, ch 1, skip next st, sc in next ch sp, (ch 1, skip next st, sc in next ch sp) across to last 2 sts, ch 1, skip next st, sc in last st, turn (40 sc, 39 ch sps).

Rows 4-88: Repeat rows 2 and 3 alternately, ending with row 2.

Rnd 89: Working in rnds, ch 1, 3 sc in first st, sc in each st and ch sp across to last st, 3 sc in last st; working in ends of rows, skip first row, sc in each of next 2 rows, skip next row, (sc in next 5 rows, skip next row) across; working in starting ch on opposite side of row 1, 3 sc in first ch, sc in each ch across to last ch, 3 sc in last ch; repeat between **, join with sl st in first sc, fasten off.

Rnd 90: Join green with sc in any st, sc in each st around with 3 sc in each center corner st, join, fasten off.

PANSY (make 18)

Row 1: With K hook and yellow, ch 4, sl st in first ch to form ring, ch 1, 3 sc in ring, fasten off (3 sc).

Row 2: With K hook and 2 strands black held together, join with sl st in ring before first sc of row 1, (sc, dc, sc, sl st) in each of next 3 sc, sl st in ring after last sc of row 1, fasten off (14 sts).

Rnd 3: Working in rnds, with K hook, join lavender with sl st in ring of row 1 after last sl st on row 2, ch 2, *(dc in ring, ch 1) 3 times, sl st in ring, ch 1; repeat from *, skip first st of last row, (sc in next st, 3 sc in next st, sc in next st, sl st in next st) 3 times, skip last st of last row, **do not** join.

Rnd 4: Sl st in next ch sp, (ch 3, sl st in next ch sp) 3 times, ch 1, sl st in next sl st between petals, ch 1, sl st in next ch sp, (ch 3, sl st in next ch sp) 3 times, leaving remaining sts unworked, fasten off.

continued on page 62

Pansies

Continued from page 61

LEAF (make 36)

With K hook and green, ch 6, sl st in 2nd ch from hook, sc in next ch, dc in next ch, sc in next ch, (sl st, ch 1, sl st) in last ch; working on opposite side of ch, sc in next ch, dc in next ch, sc in next ch, sl st in last ch, join with sl st in first sl st, fasten off.

Sew Pansies and Leaves to Afghan as shown in diagram.◆

PANSY DIAGRAM

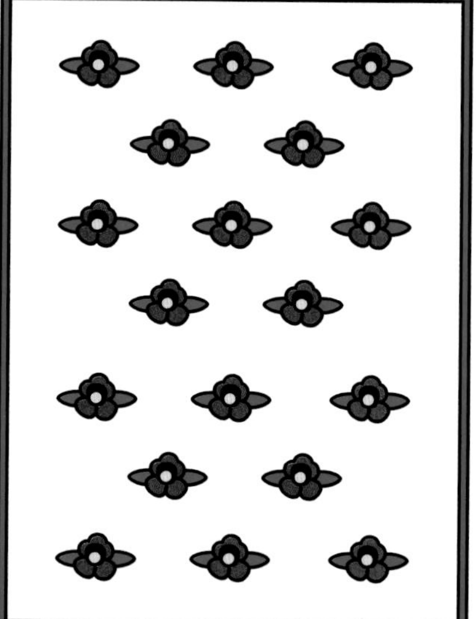

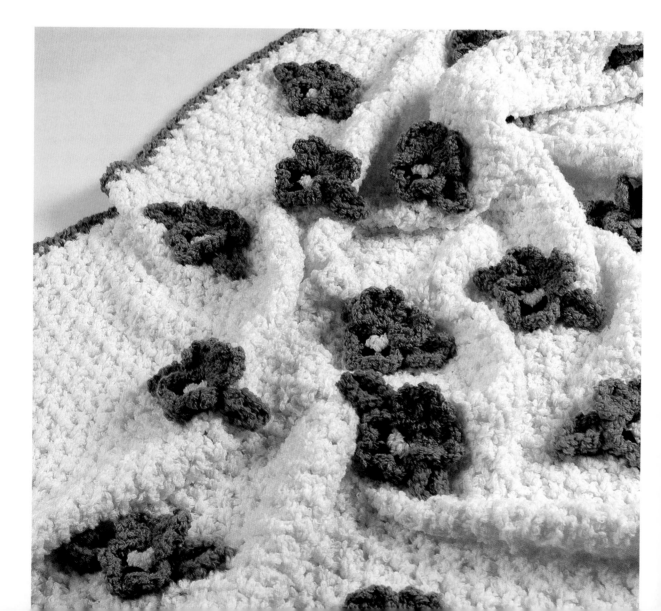

Flower Garden

Continued from page 57

***NOTE:** For **half triple treble (htr tr)**, yo 3 times, insert hook in st, yo, draw lp through, (yo, draw through 2 lps on hook) 2 times, yo, draw through all 3 lps on hook.*

Rnd 2: Join purple with sl st in any st, ch 4, (htr tr, ch 4, sl st) in same st, (sl st, ch 4, htr tr, ch 4, sl st) in each st around, join with sl st in first sl st, fasten off.

Sew one Flower to top of stem on each Block.

BORDER

Working around entire outer edge, join green with sl st in corner ch sp before one short end, beg V-st, ch 2, V-st in same sp, V-st in each V-st and in each seam around with (V-st, ch 2, V-st) in each corner ch sp, join with sl st in 3rd ch of ch-4, fasten off.◆

FLOWER GRAPH

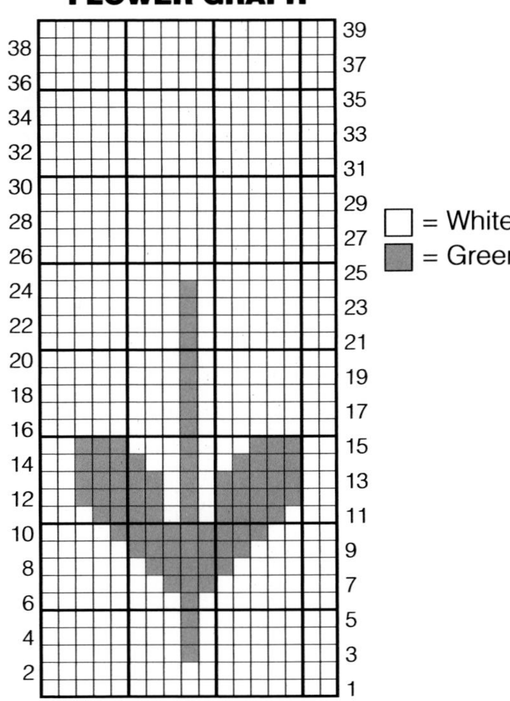

Each square on graph = 1 sc.

Add some excitement to your stitchery with extraordinary beaded curls of fringe; vibrant strips each encompassed with lacy embellishments.

Midsummer Nights

by DOT DRAKE

SIZE: 43" x 62½" not including Fringe.

MATERIALS: Worsted-weight yarn — 15 oz. white, 10 oz. purple, 5 oz. each fuschia, yellow and lavender; 70 iridescent 6-mm x 9-mm pony beads; E and G crochet hooks or size needed to obtain gauge.

GAUGE: With **G hook,** rnds 1-2 of Motif = 3" across. Each Motif is 5½" across. Each Strip is 8½" wide.

NOTE: Use G hook unless otherwise stated.

SKILL LEVEL: ☆☆☆ Advanced

FIRST STRIP

First Motif

***NOTE:** For **2-dc cluster (2-dc cl),** yo, insert hook in ch, yo, draw lp through, yo, draw through 2 lps on hook, yo, insert hook in same ch, yo, draw lp through, yo, draw through 2 lps on hook, yo, draw through all 3 lps on hook.*

Rnd 1: With white, ch 3, dc in 3rd ch from hook (first cl made), ch 2, (2-dc cl in same ch, ch 2) 5 times, join with sl st in top of first dc, fasten off (6 cls, 6 ch sps).

***NOTE:** For **3-tr cluster (3-tr cl),** yo 2 times, insert hook in next ch sp, yo, draw lp through, (yo, draw through 2 lps on hook) 2 times, *yo 2 times, insert hook in same sp, yo, draw lp through, (yo, draw through 2 lps on hook) 2 times; repeat from *, yo, draw through all 4 lps on hook.*

Rnd 2: For **petals,** join fuschia with sc in any ch sp, ch 5, (3-tr cl, ch 5, sc) in same sp, (sc, ch 5, 3-tr cl, ch 5, sc) in each ch sp around, join with sl st in first sc, fasten off (6 petals).

Rnd 3: Join white with sc in top of any cl, (ch 5, dc in 5th ch from hook) 2 times, *sc in top of next cl, (ch 5, dc in 5th ch from hook) 2 times; repeat from * around, join (12 ch sps, 6 sc).

Rnd 4: Ch 1, sc in first sc, (2 sc, ch 3, 2 sc) in next ch sp, sc in top of next dc, (2 sc, ch 3, 2 sc) in next ch sp, *sc in next sc, (2 sc, ch 3, 2 sc) in next ch sp, sc in top of next dc, (2 sc, ch 3, 2 sc) in next ch sp; repeat from * around, join, fasten off (60 dc, 12 ch sps).

Rnd 5: Join purple with sc in any ch sp, ch 6, (sc in next ch sp, ch 6) around, join (12 sc, 12 ch sps).

Rnd 6: Ch 1, sc in first st, (3 sc, ch 3, 3 sc) in next ch sp, *sc in next st, (3 sc, ch 3, 3 sc) in next ch sp; repeat from * around, join, fasten off (84 sc, 12 ch sps).

Second Motif

Rnds 1-5: Repeat same rnds of First Motif,

continued on page 66

Midsummer Nights

Continued from page 64

using lavender for petals on rnd 2.

Rnd 6: Ch 1, sc in first st, 3 sc in next ch sp; joining to center 3 ch sps on bottom of last Motif made (see Joining Diagram), ch 1, sl st in first ch sp on other Motif, ch 1, 3 sc in same ch sp on this Motif, (sc in next st, 3 sc in next ch sp, ch 1, sl st in next ch sp on other Motif, ch 1, 3 sc in same ch sp on this Motif) 2 times, *sc in next st, (3 sc, ch 3, 3 sc) in next ch sp; repeat from * around, join, fasten off.

JOINING DIAGRAM

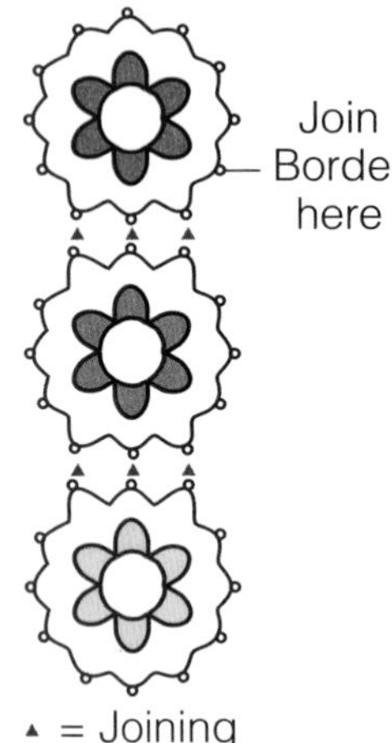

Working in color sequence of yellow, fuschia and lavender for petals on rnd 2, repeat Second Motif 9 more times, ending with lavender petals on last Motif.

Border

***NOTE:** For **decrease (dec),** skip next 3 sc, *yo 2 times, insert hook in next sc, yo, draw lp through, (yo, draw through 2 lps on hook) 2 times*, skip next 3 sc, skip next joining, skip next 3 sc; repeat between **, yo, draw through all 3 lps on hook.*

Working around outer edge, with white, ch 8, dc in 6th ch from hook, dc in each of last 2 chs; joining to Motif on one end (see diagram), ◊ch 1, sc in first unworked ch sp after joining, ch 1, **turn,** dc in each of next 3 dc, **turn,** ch 5, dc in each of next 3 dc, *ch 2, skip next 3 sc on Motif, sc in next sc, ch 2, **turn,** dc in each of next 3 dc, **turn,** ch 5, dc in each of next 3 dc, ch 1, sc in next ch sp on Motif, ch 1, **turn,** dc in each of next 3 dc, **turn,** ch 5, dc in each of next 3 dc*; repeat between ** 7 more times, dec, **turn,** [sl st in next dc, ch 3, dc in each of next 2 dc, **turn,** ch 5, dc in each of next 3 dc, ch 1, sc in next ch sp on Motif, ch 1, **turn,** dc in each of next 3 dc, **turn,** ch 5, dc in each of next 3 dc; repeat between ** 2 times, dec, **turn];** repeat between [ ] 8 more times, sl st in next dc, ch 3, dc in each of next 2 dc, **turn**◊, ch 5, dc in each of next 3 dc; repeat between ◊◊; matching sts and working through both thicknesses, sl st first and last 3 dc together, fasten off.

SECOND STRIP

First Motif

With lavender for petals on rnd 2, work same as First Strip First Motif.

Second Motif

Rnds 1-5: With fuschia for petals on rnd 2, repeat same rnds of First Strip First Motif,

Rnd 6: Repeat same rnd of First Strip Second Motif.

Working in color sequence of yellow, lavender and fuschia for petals on rnd 2, repeat Second Motif 9 more times, ending with fuschia petals on last Motif.

Border

***NOTE:** Leave 8 unworked ch-5 sps centered across each end of Strips between joinings.*

Working in the following steps:

Step A: working around outer edge, with white, ch 8, dc in 6th ch from hook, dc in each of last 2 chs; joining to Motif on one end, ch 1, sc in first unworked ch sp after joining, ch 1, **turn,** dc in each of next 3 dc, **turn,** *ch 5, dc in each of next

Midsummer Nights

Continued from page 66

3 dc, ch 2, skip next 3 sc on Motif, sc in next sc, ch 2, **turn,** dc in each of next 3 dc, **turn,** ch 5, dc in each of next 3 dc, ch 1, sc in next ch sp on Motif, ch 1, **turn,** dc in each of next 3 dc, **turn***; repeat between ** 5 more times;

Step B: joining to side of last Strip, ch 2, sc in corresponding ch-5 sp on other Strip (see Note), ch 2, **turn,** dc in each of next 3 dc on this Strip, [ch 2, skip next 3 sc on Motif, sc in next sc, ch 2, **turn,** dc in each of next 3 dc, ch 2, sc in next ch-5 sp on other Strip, ch 2, **turn,** dc in each of next 3 dc on this Strip, ch 1, sc in next ch sp on Motif, ch 1, **turn,** dc in each of next 3 dc, ch 2, sc in next ch-5 sp on other Strip, ch 2, **turn,** dc in each of next 3 dc on this Strip]; repeat between [ ];

Step C: ◊dec, **turn,** sl st in next dc, ch 3, dc in each of next 2 dc, ch 2, sc in next ch-5 sp on other Strip, ch 2, **turn,** dc in each of next 3 dc on this Strip, ch 1, sc in next ch sp on Motif, ch 1, **turn,** dc in each of next 3 dc, ch 2, sc in next ch-5 sp on other Strip, ch 2, **turn,** dc in each of next 3 dc; repeat between [ ] in Step B 2 more times; repeat from ◊ 9 more times;

Step D: •ch 2, skip next 3 sc on Motif, sc in next sc, ch 2, **turn,** dc in each of next 3 dc, **turn,** ch 5, dc in each of next 3 dc, ch 1, sc in next ch sp on Motif, ch 1, **turn,** dc in each of next 3 dc, **turn,** ch 5, dc in each of next 3 dc•; repeat between •• 5 more times, dec, **turn,** ◊sl st in next dc, ch 3, dc in each of next 2 dc, **turn,** ch 5, dc in each of next 3 dc, ch 1, sc in next ch sp on Motif, ch 1, **turn,** dc in each of next 3 dc, **turn,** ch 5, dc in each of next 3 dc; repeat between •• 2 times, dec, **turn;** repeat from ◊ 8 more times, sl st in next dc, ch 3, dc in each of next 2 dc, **turn;** matching sts and working through both thicknesses, sl st first and last 3 dc together, fasten off.

Alternating color sequence of First and Second Strips, repeat Second Strip 3 more times for a total of 5 Strips.

EDGING & FRINGE

NOTE: *Use E hook to sc through beads; use G hook for remainder of Edging & Fringe.*

Working around entire outer edge, join purple with sc in 6th ch-5 sp on one end Strip before joining, sc in same sp; for ***Fringe,*** *ch 20; with E hook, sc through one bead, change to G hook, 2 sc in 2nd ch from hook, 2 sc in each ch across; 2 sc in same sp on Strip, 2 sc in end of next row, *(2 sc, Fringe, 2 sc) in next ch-5 sp, 2 sc in end of next row*; repeat between ** 4 more times, •2 sc in each of next 2 joining ch sps, 2 sc in end of next row; [repeat between ** 8 times, 2 sc in each of next 2 joining ch sps, 2 sc in end of next row]; repeat between [ ] 2 times; repeat between ** 6 times, ◊(2 sc, ch 3, 2 sc) in next ch-5 sp, 2 sc in end of next row; repeat from ◊ around to 6th ch-5 sp before joining on end of Strip•; repeat between ** 6 times; repeat between ••, join with sl st in first sc, fasten off.*◆

Floral Bounty

Continued from page 58

2 sts) at each seam, join with sl st in first sc, fasten off.◆

ASSEMBLY DIAGRAM

Fireworks, Picnics & Sunshine

Chapter Four

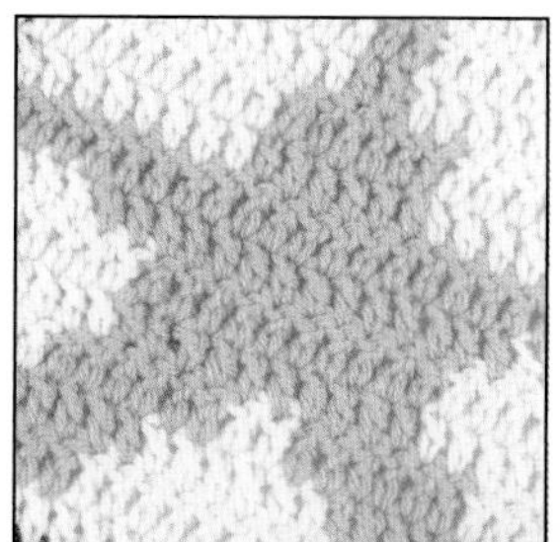

Star gazing, combined with a crafty imaginative touch, inspire easy-to-stitch designs sure to add a twinkle to starry eyes as well.

Country Star

by MAGGIE WELDON

SIZE: 49" x 65".

MATERIALS: Worsted-weight yarn — 35 oz. ecru, 14 oz. dk. blue and 3½ oz. burgundy; tapestry needle; I crochet hook or size needed to obtain gauge.

GAUGE: 7 sc = 2"; 7 sc rows = 2". Each Block is 8" square.

SKILL LEVEL: ☆☆ Average

BLOCK (make 48)

NOTES: *When changing colors (see page 159), always drop yarn to wrong side of work. Use a separate skein or ball of yarn for each color section.* ***Do not*** *carry yarn across from one section to another. Fasten off colors at end of each color section.*

Work odd-numbered graph rows from right to left and even-numbered rows from left to right.

Each square on graph equals 1 sc.

Row 1: With ecru, ch 22, sc in 2nd ch from hook, sc in each ch across, turn (21 sc).

Row 2: Ch 1, sc in each st across, turn.

Row 3: Ch 1, sc in first 6 sts changing to dk. blue in last st made, sc in next st changing to ecru, sc in next 7 sts changing to dk. blue in last st made, sc in next st changing to ecru, sc in last 6 sts, turn.

Rows 4-21: Ch 1, sc in each st across changing colors according to graph on page 77, turn. At end of last row, **do not** turn.

Rnd 22: Working around outer edge, ch 1, skip end of first row, sc in each row across to last row, skip last row; working in starting ch on opposite side of row 1, 3 sc in first ch, sc in each ch across to last ch, 3 sc in last ch, skip end of first row, sc in each row across to last row, skip last row, 3 sc in first st, sc in each st across to last st, 3 sc in last st, join with sl st in first sc, fasten off.

Rnd 23: Join dk. blue with sc in any st, sc in each st around with 3 sc in each center corner st, join, fasten off.

Rnd 24: Join ecru with sl st in any st, ch 3, dc in each st around with (2 dc, ch 2, 2 dc) in each center corner st, join with sl st in top of ch-3, fasten off.

Holding Blocks wrong sides together, matching sts, with ecru, sew together through **back lps** in 6 rows of 8 Blocks each.

BORDER

Working around entire outer edge, join ecru with sl st in any corner ch sp, ch 3, (dc, ch 2, 2 dc) in same sp, dc in each st, in each seam and in each ch sp on each side of seams around with (2 dc, ch

continued on page 77

Bordered in jet black with yellow swirls of color splashed across a background of green, these blooms really flourish.

Black-Eyed Susan

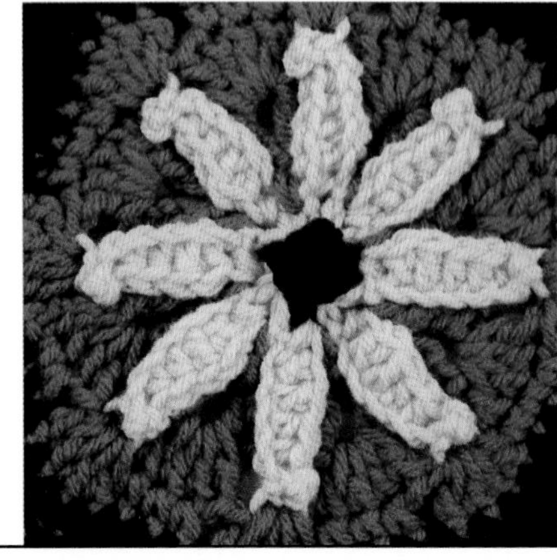

by TONYA DODSON FLYNN

SIZE: 44" x 56".

MATERIALS: Worsted-weight yarn — 25 oz. green, 15 oz. black, 8 oz. gold; tapestry needle; H crochet hook or size needed to obtain gauge.

GAUGE: Each Hexagon is 6¼" across.

SKILL LEVEL: ☆☆ Average

BACK BAR OF SC

HEXAGON (make 63)

Rnd 1: With black, ch 3, sl st in first ch to form ring; for **beginning popcorn (beg pc),** ch 3, 4 dc in ring, drop lp from hook, insert hook in top of ch-3, draw dropped lp through, fasten off (1 pc).

Rnd 2: For **first petal,** join gold with sc in top of pc, (ch 8, sc in 2nd ch from hook, sc in next ch, hdc in each of next 2 chs, dc in each of next 2 chs, hdc in last ch); for **2nd petal,** sc in same pc; repeat between ( ); for **3rd petal,** sc in end of next row; repeat between ( ); for **4th petal,** sc in same row; repeat between ( ); for **5th petal,** *sc in starting ring; repeat between ( )*; for **6th petal,** repeat between **; for **7th petal,** sc in end of next row; repeat between ( ); for **8th petal,** sc in end of same row; repeat between ( ), join with sl st in first sc, fasten off.

Rnd 3: Working behind petals in sc between petals, join green with sc in any sc, ch 4, (sc in next sc, ch 4) around, join with sl st in first sl st (8 ch sps).

Rnd 4: Sl st in first ch sp, ch 3, 3 dc in same sp, ch 1, (4 dc in next ch sp, ch 1) around, join with sl st in top of ch-3 (32 dc).

Rnd 5: Sl st in each of next 3 sts, sl st in next ch sp, ch 3, 3 dc in same sp, ch 1, sl st in **back bar** (see illustration) of sc at tip of next petal, ch 1, *4 dc in next ch sp, ch 1, sl st in back bar of sc at tip of next petal, ch 1; repeat from * around, join.

Rnd 6: Ch 1, sc in each of first 3 sts, (*skip next st; working over sl st of last rnd, 4 dc in back bar of sc on tip of next petal*, sc in each of next 3 sts) 7 times; repeat between **, join with sl st in first sc, fasten off (56 sts).

Rnd 7: Join black with sc in any st, sc in each st around, join, fasten off.

Holding Hexagons wrong sides together, matching sts, with black, sew together through **back lps** in 7 rows of 9 Hexagons each.

continued on page 77

Proudly salute our rich heritage when you lovingly stitch these majestic eagles among patriotic colors of red, white and blue.

Eagles' Ballad

by SANDRA MILLER MAXFIELD

SIZE: 60½" x 80".

MATERIALS: Worsted-weight yarn — 31½ oz. off-white, 14 oz. burgundy, 10½ oz. each brown and blue, 3½ oz. gold and white; I crochet hook or size needed to obtain gauge.

GAUGE: 3 dc = 1"; 3 dc rows = 2".

SKILL LEVEL: ☆☆ Average

AFGHAN

Row 1: With blue, ch 184, dc in 4th ch from hook, dc in each ch across, turn (182 dc).

NOTES: *When changing colors (see page 159), always drop yarn to wrong side of work. Use a separate skein or ball of yarn for each color section.* ***Do not*** *carry yarn across from one section to another. Fasten off colors at end of each color section.*

Work even-numbered graph rows from left to right and odd-numbered rows from right to left.

Each square on graph equals 2 dc.

Row 2: For **row 2 of graph,** ch 3, dc in next st changing to off-white, dc in next 178 sts changing to blue in last st made, dc in each of last 2 sts, turn.

Rows 3-120: Ch 3, dc in each st across changing colors according to graph on page 76, turn. At end of last row, fasten off.◆

continued on page 76

USA

Eagle's Ballad

Instructions on page 74

Each square on graph = 2 dc.

☐ = Off-white ■ = White
■ = Blue ■ = Burgundy
■ = Brown ■ = Gold

Country Star

Continued from page 70

2, 2 dc) in each corner ch sp, join with sl st in top of ch-3, fasten off.◆

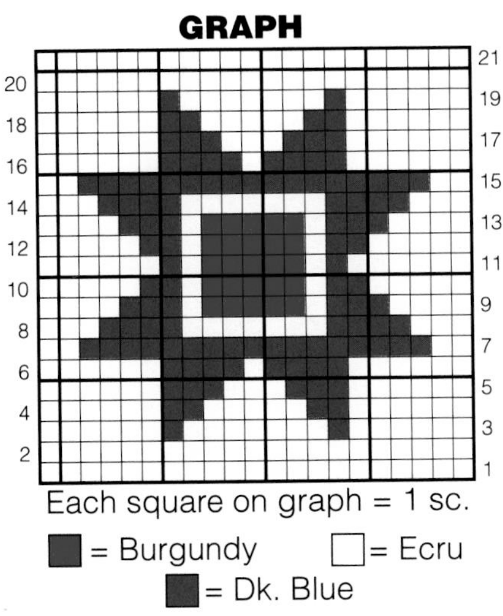

Black-Eyed Susan

Continued from page 73

FILLER MOTIF (make 48)

Rnd 1: With black, ch 3, sl st in first ch to form ring, ch 3, 2 dc in ring, ch 1, (3 dc in ring, ch 1) 3 times, join with sl st in top of ch-3 (4 ch sps).

Rnd 2: Sl st in each of next 2 sts, sl st in next ch sp, ch 3, (2 dc, ch 1, 3 dc) in same sp, ch 1, *(3 dc, ch 1, 3 dc) in next ch sp, ch 1; repeat from * 2 more times, join, fasten off.

Working in spaces between Hexagons, matching sts, with black, sew one Filler Motif to each space through **back lps**.◆

Enjoy triple waves of stunning shades as simple shell stitches boisterously zig-zag their way across.

Rippling Reflections

by HAZEL OSBURN JONES

SIZE: 46" x 60".

MATERIALS: Worsted-weight yarn — 14 oz. black, 5 oz. each pink, rose, burgundy, yellow, lt. gold, dk. gold, lt. blue, med. blue and dk. blue; I crochet hook or size needed to obtain gauge.

GAUGE: 3 shells = 2"; 4 shell rows = 1½".

SKILL LEVEL: ☆☆ Average

AFGHAN

***NOTE:** For **shell**, (sc, ch 2, sc) in next ch or ch sp.*

Row 1: With black, ch 342, sc in 2nd ch from hook, skip next ch, shell in next ch, (skip next 2 chs, shell in next ch) 4 times, *skip next 2 chs, (shell, ch 3, shell) in next ch, (skip next 2 chs, shell in next ch) 4 times, skip next 2 chs, sc in next ch, skip next 3 chs, sc in next ch, (skip next 2 chs, shell in next ch) 4 times; repeat from * 8 more times, skip next 2 chs, (shell, ch 3, shell) in next ch, (skip next 2 chs, shell in next ch) 5 times, skip next ch, sc in last ch, turn.

Row 2: Ch 1, sc in first st, sc in ch sp of next shell, shell in ch sp of next 5 shells, *(shell, ch 3, shell) in next ch-3 sp, shell in ch sp of next 4 shells, sc in ch sp of each of next 2 shells skipping sc between, shell in ch sp of next 4 shells; repeat from * 8 more times, (shell, ch 3, shell) in next ch-3 sp, shell in ch sp of next 5 shells, sc in ch sp of next shell leaving last st or sts unworked, turn, fasten off.

Row 3: Join yellow with sc in first st, sc in next shell, shell in next 5 shells, *(shell, ch 3, shell) in next ch-3 sp, shell in next 4 shells, sc in each of next 2 shells skipping sc between, shell in next 4 shells; repeat from * 8 more times, (shell, ch 3, shell) in next ch-3 sp, shell in next 5 shells, sc in next shell leaving last st or sts unworked, turn.

Row 4: Repeat row 2.

Rows 5-74: Working in color sequence of lt. gold, dk. gold, black, pink, rose, burgundy, black, lt. blue, med. blue, dk. blue, black, yellow, repeat rows 3 and 4 alternately, ending with black. At end of last row, **do not** fasten off.

Rnd 75: Working in rnds, ch 1, sc in first st, sc in next shell, shell in next 5 shells, *(shell, ch 3, shell) in next ch-3 sp, shell in next 4 shells, sc in each of next 2 shells skipping sc between, shell in next 4 shells; repeat from * 8 more times, (shell, ch 3, shell) in next ch-3 sp, shell in next 5 shells, sc in next shell; working in ends of rows, evenly space 70 shells across; working in starting ch on opposite side of row 1, sc in first ch, shell in ch at base of next 5 shells, ◊2 sc in ch at base of (shell, ch 3, shell), shell in ch at base of next 4 shells, (shell, ch

continued on page 83

Assembled as you work, these profuse patches of flora grandly display a variety of unique joining techniques.

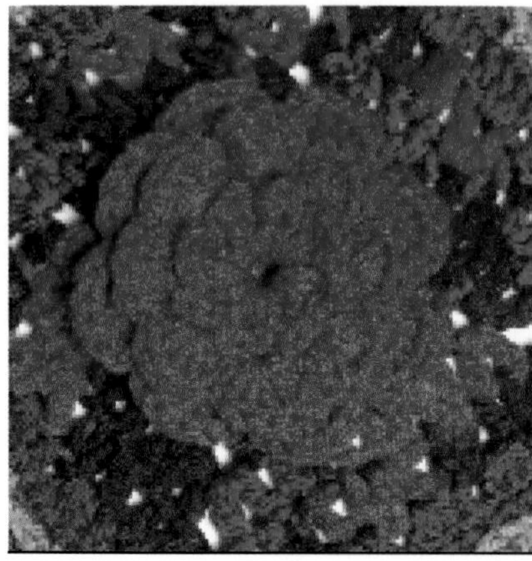

Princess Patchwork

by MARGRET WILLSON

SIZE: 48½" x 61½".

MATERIALS: Worsted-weight yarn — 20 oz. teal green, 12 oz. each pink and variegated, 10 oz. purple and 8 oz. gold; H crochet hook or size needed to obtain gauge.

GAUGE: 4 dc = 1". Each Block is 6½" square.

SKILL LEVEL: ☆☆☆ Advanced

MOTIF BLOCK (make 32)
First Motif

NOTE: *For* ***beginning 4-dc cluster (beg 4-dc cl),*** *ch 2, (yo, insert hook in same sp, yo, draw lp through, yo, draw through 2 lps on hook) 3 times, yo, draw through all 4 lps on hook.*

For ***4-dc cluster (4-dc cl),*** *yo, insert hook in next ch sp, yo, draw lp through, yo, draw through 2 lps on hook, (yo, insert hook in same sp, yo, draw lp through, yo, draw through 2 lps on hook) 3 times, yo, draw through all 5 lps on hook.*

Rnd 1: With pink, ch 4, sl st in first ch to form ring, ch 4, (dc in ring, ch 1) 7 times, join with sl st in 3rd ch of ch-4 (8 ch sps).

Rnd 2: Sl st in next ch sp, beg 4-dc cl, ch 3, (4-dc cl in next ch sp, ch 3) around, join with sl st in top of beg cl, fasten off.

Rnd 3: Join teal green with sl st in any ch sp, ch 3, (2 dc, ch 3, 3 dc) in same sp, 3 dc in next ch sp, *(3 dc, ch 3, 3 dc) in next ch sp, 3 dc in next ch sp; repeat from * around, join with sl st in top of ch-3, fasten off (9 dc across each side between corner ch sps).

Rnd 4: Join gold with sc in any corner ch sp, ch 3, sc in same sp, *[ch 3, (skip next 3 sts, sc in sp between last skipped st and next st, ch 3) 2 times], (3 dc, ch 3, 3 dc) in next corner ch sp; repeat from * 2 more times; repeat between [ ], join with sl st in first sc, fasten off (3 ch sps across each side between center corner ch sps).

Second Motif

Rnd 1: With purple, repeat same rnd of First Motif.

Rnds 2-3: Repeat same rnds of First Motif.

NOTE: *For* ***joining ch 3,*** *ch 1, sl st in corresponding ch sp on other Motif or Block, ch 1.*

Rnd 4: Join gold with sc in any corner ch sp, joining to side of last Motif, work joining ch 3, sc in same sp on this Motif, (work joining ch 3, skip next 3 sts on this Motif, sc in sp between last skipped st and next st) 2 times, work joining ch 3, 3 dc in next corner ch sp on this Motif, work joining ch 3, sc in same sp on this Motif, *[ch 3, (skip next 3 sts, sc in sp between last skipped st and

continued on page 82

Princess Patchwork

Continued from page 80

next st, ch 3) 2 times], (sc, ch 3, sc) in next corner ch sp, repeat from *; repeat between [ ], join with sl st in first sc, fasten off.

Third Motif

Joining to bottom of First Motif, work same as Second Motif on page 80.

Fourth Motif

Rnds 1-3: Repeat same rnds of First Motif on page 80.

Rnd 4: Join gold with sc in any corner ch sp; joining to bottom of Second Motif, work joining ch 3, sc in same sp on this Motif, *work joining ch 3, (skip next 3 sts on this Motif, sc in sp between last skipped st and next st, work joining ch 3) 2 times, 3 dc in next corner ch sp on this Motif, work joining ch 3, 3 dc in same sp on this Motif*; joining to side of Third Motif, repeat between **, [ch 3, (skip next 3 sts, sc in sp between last skipped st and next st, ch 3) 2 times], (sc, ch 2, sc) in next corner ch sp; repeat between [ ], join with sl st in first sc, fasten off.

FLOWER BLOCK (make 17 with pink Flower, 14 with purple Flower)

NOTES: Work and join Blocks according to Assembly Diagram working rnds 1-6 of Flower Block in color indicated on diagram.

*For **2-dc cluster (2-dc cl),** (yo, insert hook in sp, yo, draw lp through, yo, draw through 2 lps on hook) 2 times, yo, draw through all 3 lps on hook.*

Rnd 1: With flower color, ch 5, sl st in first ch to form ring, (ch 2, 2-dc cl in ring, ch 2, sc in ring) 8 times, **do not** join (8 petals).

2 BACK STRANDS OF SC

Rnd 2: Working behind petals, *ch 3, sc in **back strands** (see illustration) of next sc; repeat from * around (8 ch sps).

Rnd 3: Sl st in next ch sp, ch 1, sc in same ch sp, *5 dc in next sc, sc in next ch-3 sp) 7 times, 5 dc in last sc, sc in back strands of first sc.

Rnd 4: Repeat row 2.

Rnd 5: Sl st in next ch sp, ch 1, sc in same sp, (7 dc in next sc, sc in next ch-3 sp) 7 times, 7 dc in last sc, sc in back strands of first sc.

Rnd 6: Repeat row 2, fasten off.

*NOTE: For **V-stitch (V-st),** (dc, ch 1, dc) in next st or sp.*

Rnd 7: Join variegated with sl st in any sc, ch 4, (dc, ch 2, V-st) in same st, *[dc in next ch sp, V-st in next st, dc in next ch sp], (V-st, ch 2, V-st) in next st; repeat from * 2 more times; repeat between [ ], join with sl st in 3rd ch of ch-4 (3 V-sts and 2 dc across each side between corner ch sps).

Rnd 8: Sl st in next ch sp, ch 3, *(V-st, ch 3, V-st) in next corner ch sp, dc in ch sp of next V-st, (skip next st, V-st in next st, dc in ch sp of next V-st) 2 times; repeat from * 2 more times, (V-st, ch 3, V-st) in next corner ch sp, (dc in ch sp of next V-st, skip next st, V-st in next st) 2 times, join with sl st in top of ch-3 (4 V-sts and 3 dc across each side between corner ch sps).

Rnd 9: Ch 4, dc in same st, dc in next V-st, *[(V-st, ch 3, V-st) in next ch sp, dc in next V-st, skip next st], (V-st in next st, dc in next V-st, skip next st) 3 times; repeat from * 2 more times; repeat between [ ], (V-st in next st, dc in next V-st, skip next st) 2 times, join with sl st in 3rd ch of ch-4, fasten off (5 V-sts and 4 dc across each side between corner ch sps).

Rnd 10: Join teal green with sl st in any corner ch sp, ch 3, (2 dc, ch 3, 3 dc) in same sp, *[3 dc in next V-st, (skip next st, dc in next st, 3 dc in next V-st) across] to next corner ch sp, (3 dc, ch 3, 3 dc) in next sp; repeat from * 2 more times; repeat between [ ], join with sl st in top of ch-3, fasten off (25 dc across each side between corner ch sps).

Three-Side Joined Flower Block

*NOTES: For **joining edge,** work joining ch 3, skip next 3 sts on this Block, sc in sp between last skipped st and next st, (joining ch 3, skip next 3 sts on this Block, sc in next st) 2 times, ch 1, sl st in next joining on other Block, ch 1, skip next 3 sts on this Block, sc in next st, ch 1, skip ch sp after joining on other Block, sl st in next ch sp, ch 1, skip next 3 sts on this Block, sc in next st, joining ch 3, skip next 3 sts on this Block, sc in sp between last skipped st and next st, joining ch 3, skip next 3 sts on this Block, sc in next corner ch sp, joining ch 3, sc in same sp on this Block.*

Flower Blocks and Motif Blocks are same in actual size. The Flower Blocks in the following Graphs are smaller than Motif Blocks to allow room for directional arrows.

Joining Flower Block to side of Motif Block (see Three-Side Joined Diagram), join gold with sc in

THREE-SIDE JOINED DIAGRAM

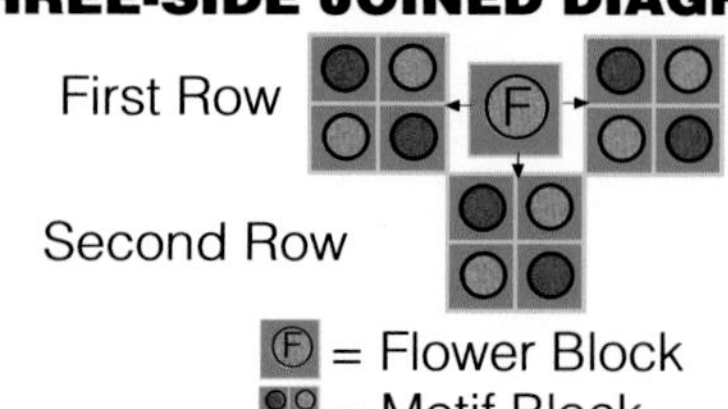

any corner ch sp on Flower Block, joining ch 3, sc in same sp on this Block, work joining edge; *joining same Flower Block to side of next Motif Block, work joining edge; repeat from *, ch 3, skip next 3 sts, sc in sp between last skipped st and next st, ch 3, skip next 3 sts, (sc in next st, ch 3, skip next 3 sts) 4 times, sc in sp between last skipped st and next st, ch 3, skip next 3 sts, join with sl st in first sc, fasten off (7 ch sps across each side between corner ch sps).

Four-Side Joined Flower Block

Joining Flower Block to side of Motif Block (see Four-Side Joined Diagram), join gold with sc in any

FOUR-SIDE JOINED DIAGRAM

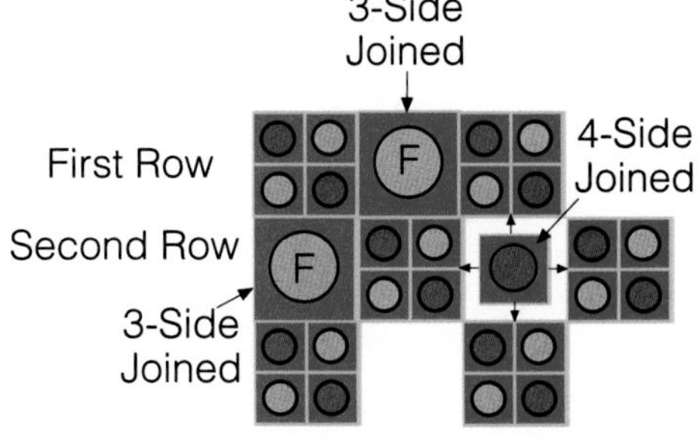

corner ch sp on Flower Block, joining ch 3, sc in same sp on this Block, work joining edge; *joining to side of next Motif Block, work joining edge; repeat from * 2 more times, joining ch 3, skip next 3 sts on this Block, sc in sp between last skipped st and next st, (joining ch 3, skip next 3 sts on this Block, sc in next st) 2 times, ch 1, sl st in next joining on other Block, ch 1, skip next 3 sts on this Block, sc in next st, ch 1, skip ch sp after joining on other Block, sl st in next ch sp, ch 1, skip next 3 sts on this Block, sc in next st, joining ch 3, skip next 3 sts on this Block, sc in sp between last skipped st and next st, joining ch 3, skip next 3 sts on this Block, join with sl st in first sc, fasten off (7 ch sps across each side between corner ch sps).

Join Flower and Motif Blocks according to Assembly Diagram.

ASSEMBLY DIAGRAM

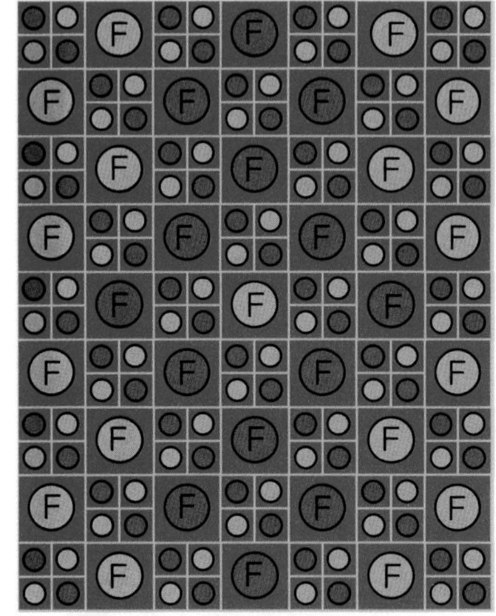

= Pink Flower Block
= Purple Flower Block
= Motif Block

BORDER

Rnd 1: Working around entire outer edge in ch sps and in each ch sp on each side of seams, join gold with sc in any corner ch sp, ch 3, sc in same sp, *[ch 3, (sc in next ch sp, ch 3) across to next corner ch sp], (sc, ch 3, sc) in next ch sp; repeat from * 2 more times; repeat between [ ], join with sl st in first sc, fasten off.

Rnd 2: Join teal green with sl st in any corner ch sp, ch 3, (2 dc, ch 3, 3 dc) in same sp, 3 dc in each ch sp around with (3 dc, ch 3, 3 dc) in each corner ch sp, join with sl st in top of ch-3, fasten off.

Rnd 3: Join pink with sc in any corner ch sp, ch 3, sc in same sp, (sc, ch 3, sc) in sp between each 3-dc group around with (sc, ch 3, sc) in each corner ch sp, join with sl st in first sc, fasten off.

Rnd 4: Join teal green with sl st in any corner ch sp, ch 3, (2 dc, ch 3, 3 dc) in same sp, 3 dc in each ch sp around with (3 dc, ch 3, 3 dc) in each corner ch sp, join with sl st in top of ch-3, fasten off.◆

Rippling Reflections

Continued from page 79

3, shell) in next ch-3 sp, shell in ch at base of next 4 shells; repeat from ◊ 8 more times, 2 sc in ch at base of (shell, ch 3, shell), shell in ch at base of next 5 shells, sc in last ch; working in ends of rows, evenly space 70 shells across, join with sl st in first sc, **turn.**

Rnd 76: Shell in next 70 shells, shell in next sc, shell in next 4 shells, *sc in each of next 2 shells skipping sc between, shell in next 4 shells, (shell, ch 3, shell) in next ch-3 sp, sc in next 4 shells; repeat from * 8 more times, sc in each of next 2 shells skipping sc between, shell in next 4 shells, shell in next sc, shell in next 70 shells, sl st in next sc, shell in next 6 shells, ◊(shell, ch 3, shell) in next ch-3 sp, shell in next 4 shells, sc in each of next 2 shells skipping sc between, shell in next 4 shells; repeat from ◊ 8 more times, (shell, ch 3, shell) in next ch-3 sp, shell in next 6 shells, sl st in last sc, join with sl st in joining sl st of last rnd, fasten off.◆

Combine this unique mix of double crochet and afghan stitch to create a stunning diamond-shaped pattern.

Diamond Daze

by DIANE POELLOT

SIZE: 50" x 66".

MATERIALS: Worsted-weight yarn — 54 oz. purple; J crochet hook or size needed to obtain gauge.

GAUGE: 1 block = 1¼" square.

SKILL LEVEL: ☆☆ Average

Row 1: Ch 164, 4 dc in 4th ch from hook, skip next 3 chs, sc in next ch, (skip next 3 chs, 9 dc in next ch, skip next 3 chs, sc in next ch) across to last 4 chs, skip next 3 chs, 5 dc in last ch, turn (201 sts).

Row 2: Working this row in **back lps** only, ch 1, sc in first st; for **block,** [pull up lp in next 5 sts (6 lps on hook), insert hook in next dc, yo, draw through st and 1 lp on hook, (yo, draw through 2 lps on hook) 5 times (1 lp on hook); *skip first vertical bar, draw up lp in next 5 vertical bars, insert hook in next dc, yo, draw through st and 1 lp on hook, (yo, draw through 2 lps on hook) 5 times; repeat from * 2 more times, skip first vertical bar, sl st in next 5 vertical bars, sc in next dc]; repeat between [ ] across, turn.

***NOTES:** For **dc next 5 sts tog,** (yo, insert hook in next st or end of row on block, yo, draw lp through, yo, draw through 2 lps on hook) 5 times, yo, draw through all 6 lps on hook; for **eye,** ch 1.*

*For **dc next 9 sts tog,** (yo, insert hook in next st or end of row on block, yo, draw lp through, yo, draw through 2 lps on hook) 9 times, yo, draw through all 10 lps on hook; for **eye,** ch 1.*

Row 3: Working this row in **front lps** only, ch 3, dc next 5 sts tog, (ch 3, sc in next st or row, ch 3, dc next 9 sts tog) across to last 5 sts or rows, ch 4, sc in end of next row, ch 3, dc same row and last 4 rows tog, turn.

Row 4: Ch 3, 4 dc in eye of first st, (skip next ch sp, sc in next sc, skip next ch sp, 9 dc in eye of next st) across to last 2 sts and 2 ch sps, sc in next sc, 5 dc in eye of last st, **do not** turn, fasten off.

Row 5: Working this row in **back lps** only, join with sc in first st; for **block,** [pull up lp in next 5 sts (6 lps on hook), insert hook in next dc, yo, draw through st and 1 lp on hook, (yo, draw through 2 lps on hook) 5 times (1 lp on hook); *skip first vertical bar, draw up lp in next 5 vertical bars, insert hook in next dc, yo, draw through st and 1 lp on hook, (yo, draw through 2 lps on hook) 5 times; repeat from * 2 more times, skip first vertical bar, sl st in next 5 vertical bars, sc in next dc]; repeat between [ ] across, turn.

Rows 6-78: Repeat rows 3-5 consecutively, ending with row 3.

continued on page 88

Add an impressive elegance to any room with strips made in sumptuous shades of blue and charming scalloped edges.

Victorian Blues

by MARGRET WILLSON

SIZE: 57" x 70".

MATERIALS: Worsted-weight yarn — 24 oz. med. blue, 21 oz. variegated, 12 oz. dk. blue and 10 oz. lt. blue; H crochet hook or size needed to obtain gauge.

GAUGE: 2 dc and 2 pc = 1¾"; rows 1-2 = 1¼". Each Strip is 5" wide.

SKILL LEVEL: ☆☆ Average

FIRST STRIP

NOTES: *For* ***popcorn (pc),*** *5 dc in next st, drop lp from hook, insert hook in first st of 5-dc group, draw dropped lp through.*

For ***V-stitch (V-st),*** *(dc, ch 1, dc) in next sp or st.*

Row 1: With variegated, ch 10, V-st in 7th ch from hook, ch 1, dc in last ch, turn (2 dc, 1 V-st).

Row 2: Ch 4, (pc in next dc, ch 1) 2 times, dc in last dc, turn (3 ch sps, 2 pc, 2 dc). Front of row 2 is right side of work.

Row 3: Ch 4, skip first ch sp, V-st in next ch sp, ch 1, dc in last st, turn (2 dc, 1 V-st).

Rows 4-104: Repeat rows 2 and 3 alternately, ending with row 2, turn.

Row 105: Ch 5, dc next 2 pc tog, ch 2, dc in last st, turn, fasten off (2 ch sps).

Rnd 106: Working around outer edge, join med. blue with sl st in first ch sp of last row, ch 3, (2 dc, ch 3, 3 dc) in same ch sp, (3 dc, ch 3, 3 dc) in next ch sp, *skip end of first row, 2 dc in end of each row across to last row, skip last row*; working in starting ch on opposite side of row 1, (3 dc, ch 3, 3 dc) in each of next 2 ch sps; repeat between **, join with sl st in top of ch-3, fasten off (6 dc across each short end between corner ch sps; 212 dc across each long edge between corner ch sps).

Rnd 107: Join lt. blue with sl st in first corner ch sp, ch 2, (2 hdc, ch 3, 3 hdc) in same sp, *sc in center st of next 3-dc group, hdc in sp between last 3-dc group and next 3-dc group, sc in center st of next 3-dc group, (3 hdc, ch 3, 3 hdc) in next corner ch sp, sc in center st of next 3-dc group, skip next 2 sts, 3 dc in sp between last skipped st and next st, (skip next 2 sts, sc in sp between last skipped st and next st, skip next 2 sts, 3 dc in sp between last skipped st and next st) across to last 3-dc group before next corner ch sp, sc in center st of 3-dc group*, (3 hdc, ch 3, 3 hdc) in next corner ch sp; repeat between **, join with sl st in top of ch-2, fasten off.

NOTE: *For* ***dc back post (bp,*** *see page 159), yo, insert hook from back to front around post of next st, yo, draw lp through, complete as dc.*

Rnd 108: Join dk. blue with sl st in first corner

continued on page 88

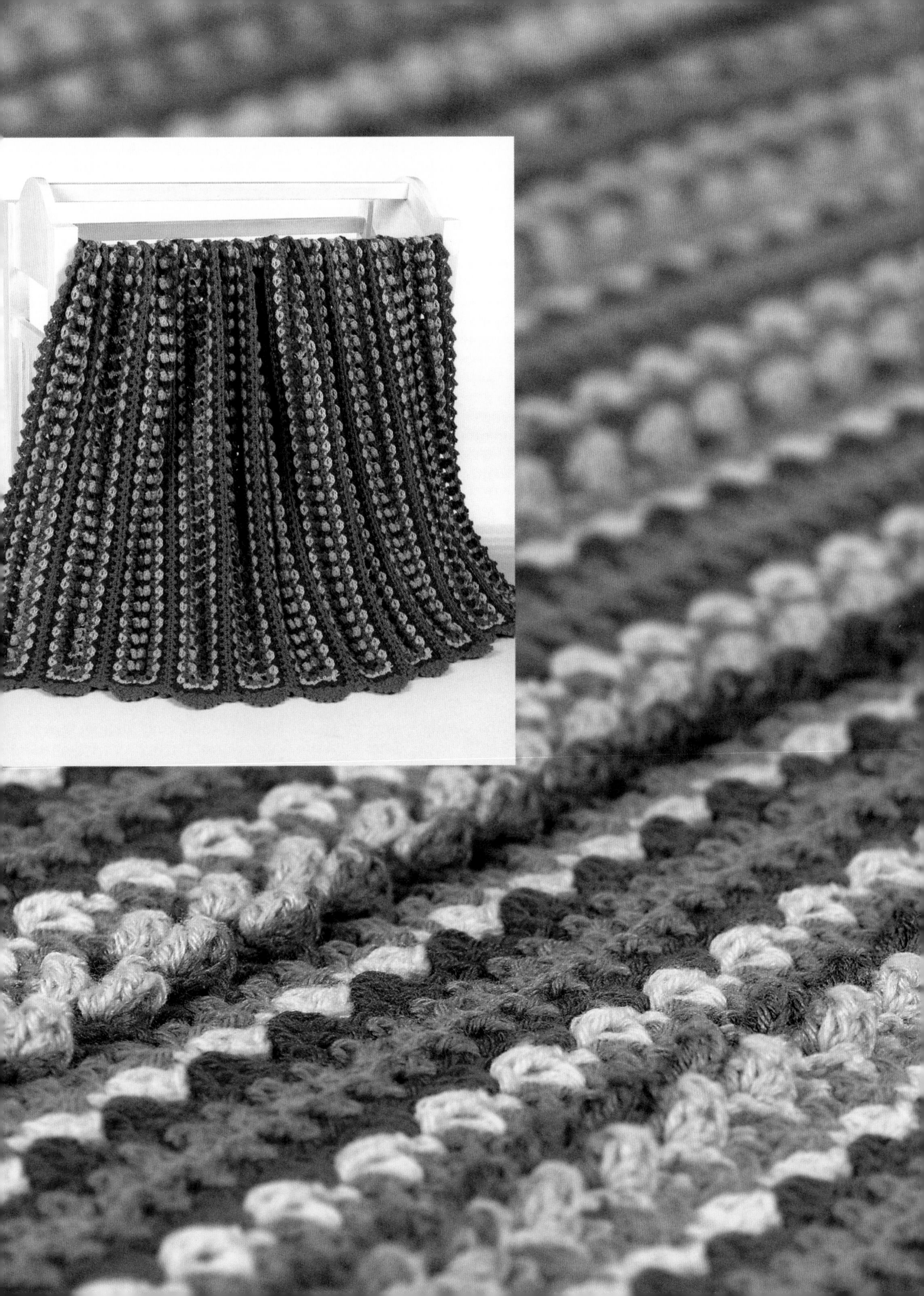

Victorian Blues

Continued from page 86

ch sp, ch 2, (2 hdc, ch 3, 3 hdc) in same sp, *sc in center st of next 3-hdc group, skip next hdc and sc, 5 dc in next hdc, sc in center st of next 3-hdc group, (3 hdc, ch 3, 3 hdc) in next corner ch sp, sc in center st of next 3-hdc group, 3 dc in next sc, (bp around center st of next 3-dc group, 3 dc in next sc) across to last 3-hdc group before next corner ch sp, sc in center st of next 3-hdc group*, (3 hdc, ch 3, 3 hdc) in next corner ch sp; repeat between **, join with sl st in top of ch-2, fasten off.

NOTES: *For* ***picot,*** *ch 3, sc in top of last st made.*

For ***picot shell,*** *dc in next st, (picot, dc in same st) 5 times.*

Rnd 109: Join med. blue with sc in first corner ch sp, ch 3, sc in same sp, *ch 3, sc in center st of next 3-hdc group, picot shell in center st of next 5-dc group, sc in center st of next 3-hdc group, ch 3, (sc, ch 3, sc) in next corner ch sp, ch 3, sc in center st of next 3-hdc group, ch 3, (sc in next sc or bp, ch 3, sc in center st of next 3-dc or 3-hdc group, ch 3) across* to next corner ch sp, (sc, ch 3, sc) in next corner ch sp; repeat between **, join with sl st in first sc, fasten off.

NEXT STRIP

Rows/Rnds 1-108: Repeat same rows/rnds of First Strip on page 86.

NOTE: *For* ***joined ch-3 sp,*** *ch 1, sl st in corresponding ch-3 sp on other Strip, ch 1.*

Rnd 109: Join med. blue with sc in first corner ch sp, ch 3, sc in same sp, *ch 3, sc in center st of next 3-hdc group, picot shell in center st of next 5-dc group, sc in center st of next 3-hdc group, ch 3*, sc in next corner ch sp; joining to last Strip made, work joined ch-3 sp, sc in same sp on this Strip, work joined ch-3 sp, sc in center st of next 3-hdc group on this Strip, work joined ch-3 sp, (sc in next sc or bp on this Strip, work joined ch-3 sp, sc in center st of next 3-dc or 3-hdc group on this Strip, work joined ch-3 sp) across to next corner ch sp, sc in next corner ch sp on this Strip, work joined ch-3 sp, sc in same sp on this Strip; repeat between **, (sc, ch 3, sc) in next corner ch sp, ch 3, sc in center st of next 3-hdc group, ch 3, (sc in next sc or bp, ch 3, sc in center st of next 3-dc or 3-hdc group, ch 3) across, join with sl st in first sc, fasten off.

Repeat Next Strip 9 more times for a total of 11 Strips.

EDGING

NOTES: *For* ***beginning picot cluster (beg picot cl),*** *ch 3, (yo, insert hook in same st or sp, yo, draw lp through, yo, draw through 2 lps on hook) 4 times, yo, draw lp through all 5 lps on hook, picot.*

For ***picot cluster (cl),*** *yo, insert hook in next st or sp, yo, draw lp through, yo, draw through 2 lps on hook, (yo, insert hook in same st or sp, yo, draw lp through, yo, draw through 2 lps on hook) 4 times, yo, draw lp through all 6 lps on hook, picot.*

Working around outer edge, join med. blue with sl st in corner ch sp before one short end, (beg picot cl, ch 2, sc, ch 2, picot cl) in same sp, ◊*[ch 2, sc in next ch sp, (dc, picot) in each of next 2 dc on next picot shell, (dc, picot) 2 times in each of next 2 dc on same picot shell, (dc, picot) in each of next 2 dc on same shell, sc in next ch sp, ch 2], picot cl in next joining; repeat from * 9 more times; repeat between [ ], (picot cl, ch 2, sc, ch 2, picot cl) in next corner ch sp, ch 2, sc in next sc, ch 2, (picot cl in next sc, ch 2, sc in next sc, ch 2) across◊ to next corner ch sp, (picot cl, ch 2, sc, ch 2, picot cl) in next corner ch sp; repeat between ◊◊, join with sl st in first picot cl, fasten off. ◆

Diamond Daze

Continued from page 85

Rnd 79: Working around outer edge, repeat row 4 ending with 13 dc in last eye; working down side of afghan, *sc in st at corner of next block, (9 dc in next eye, sc in st at corner of next block) across*; working in starting ch on opposite side of row 1, 13 dc in ch at base of next 5-dc group, sc in ch at base of next sc, (9 dc in ch at base of next 9-dc group, sc in ch at base of next sc) across, 13 dc in ch at base of last 5-dc group; working up side of afghan, repeat between **, 8 dc in same eye as first ch-3, join with sl st in top of ch-3, fasten off. ◆

Moonlight, Mischief & Magic

Chapter Five

5

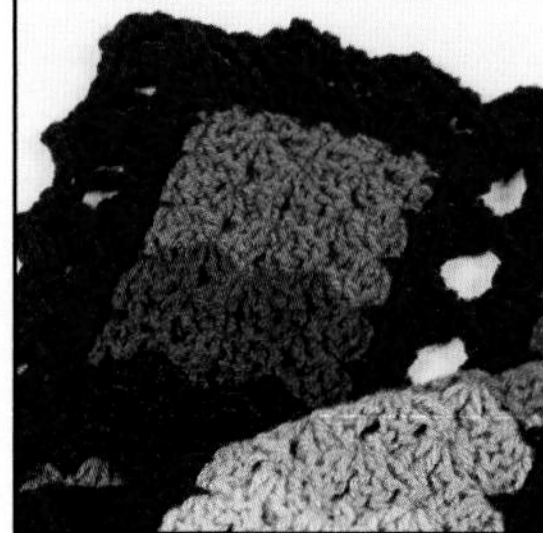

Create an unusual beaded illusion around multicolored panels using simple variations of basic stitches and vibrant hues.

Butterscotch & Caramel

by ELEANOR ALBANO-MILES

SIZE: 50½" x 68".

MATERIALS: Worsted-weight yarn — 25 oz. gold, 15 oz. each teal and rust; tapestry needle; I crochet hook or size needed to obtain gauge.

GAUGE: 7 dc = 2"; 2 dc rows and 2 sc rows = 1¾". Each Panel is 8¼" wide.

SKILL LEVEL: ☆☆ Average

PANEL (make 6)

Rnd 1: With gold, ch 196, dc in 4th ch from hook, dc in each ch across to last ch, 7 dc in last ch; working on opposite side of ch, dc in each ch across to last ch, 5 dc in last ch, join with sl st in top of ch-3, **turn** (396 dc).

Rnd 2: Ch 1, (sc, ch 2, sc) in first st, *sc in each of next 3 sts, (sc, ch 2, sc) in next st, sc in next 193 sts*, (sc, ch 2, sc) in next st; repeat between **, join with sl st in first sc, **do not** turn, fasten off (5 sc across each short end between corner ch-2 sps, 195 sc across each long edge between corner ch-2 sps). Front of rnd 2 is right side of work.

Rnd 3: Join teal with sl st in any st, ch 2, hdc in each st around with (hdc, ch 2, hdc) in each corner ch sp, join with sl st in top of ch-2, **turn,** fasten off (7 hdc across each short end between corner ch-2 sps, 197 hdc across each long edge between corner ch-2 sps).

Rnd 4: Join rust with sc in any corner ch sp, (tr, sc) in same sp, *[tr in next st, (sc in next st, tr in next st) across] to next corner ch sp, (sc, tr, sc) in next ch sp; repeat from * 2 more times; repeat between [ ], join with sl st in first sc, **turn,** fasten off.

*NOTE: For **long half double crochet (lhdc);** working over next st on last rnd, yo, insert hook in corresponding st on rnd before last, yo, draw up long lp, yo, draw through all 3 lps on hook.*

Rnd 5: Join teal with sl st in any corner tr, ch 4, hdc in same st, *[lhdc, (hdc in next st on last rnd, lhdc) across] to next corner tr on last rnd, (hdc, ch 2, hdc) in next tr; repeat from * 2 more times; repeat between [ ], join with sl st in 2nd ch of ch-4, **turn,** fasten off.

Rnd 6: With gold, repeat rnd 3.

Rnd 7: With rust, repeat rnd 3.

Rnd 8: With teal, repeat rnd 4.

Rnd 9: With rust, repeat rnd 5.

Rnd 10: With gold, repeat rnd 3, **do not** fasten off.

Rnd 11: Ch 2, hdc in each st around with (hdc, ch 2, hdc) in each corner ch sp, join with sl st in top of ch-2, fasten off (23 hdc across each short end between corner ch-2 sps, 213 hdc across each long edge between corner ch-2 sps).

continued on page 108

A multi-hued original everytime, this creative work of art is crafted almost entirely out of leftover scrap yarn.

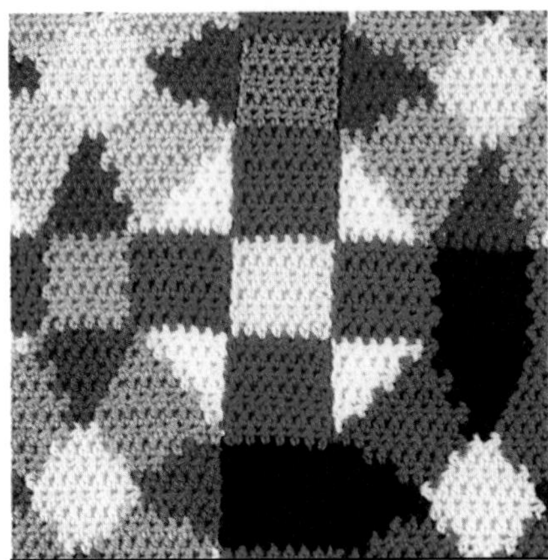

Fall Prisms

by DARLA FANTON

SIZE: 44" x 69½".

MATERIALS: Worsted-weight yarn — 19 oz. green, 8 oz. lt. yellow, 6 oz. white, 13 oz. assorted scrap yarn in light colors, 9 oz. assorted scrap yarn in dark colors (each large block requires approximately 18 yds. lt. colored scrap color and 12 yds. dk. colored scrap color and each small square requires approximately 5 yds. any scrap color); tapestry needle; H crochet hook or size needed to obtain gauge.

GAUGE: 13 hdc = 4"; 11 hdc rows = 4".

SKILL LEVEL: ☆☆ Average

SIDE STRIP (make 2)

Row 1: With green, ch 8, hdc in 3rd ch from hook, hdc in each ch across, turn (7 hdc).

Rows 2-188: Ch 2, hdc in each st across, turn. At end of last row, fasten off.

CENTER STRIP (make 4)

Row 1: With green, ch 8, hdc in 3rd ch from hook, hdc in each ch across, turn (7 hdc).

Rows 2-13: Ch 1, sc in each st across, turn. At end of last row, fasten off.

Row 14: Join scrap color with sl st in first st, ch 2, hdc in each st across, turn.

Rows 15-19: Ch 2, hdc in each st across, turn. At end of last row, fasten off.

Row 20: Join green with sl st in first st, ch 2, hdc in each st across, turn.

Rows 21-26: Ch 2, hdc in each st across, turn. At end of last row, fasten off.

Row 27: Join lt. yellow with sl st in first st, ch 2, hdc in each st across, turn.

Rows 28-32: Ch 2, hdc in each st across, turn. At end of last row, fasten off.

Row 33: Repeat row 20.

Rows 34-39: Ch 2, hdc in each st across, turn. At end of last row, fasten off.

Rows 40-175: Repeat rows 14-39 consecutively, ending with row 19.

Row 176: Repeat row 20.

Rows 177-188: Ch 2, hdc in each st across, turn. At end of last row, fasten off.

PRISM STRIP

NOTES: *Each square on graph equals one hdc.*

Beginning ch-2 is used and counted as first st.

When changing colors (see illustration on page 97), always drop yarn to wrong side of work. Use a separate skein of yarn for each color section. ***Do not*** *carry yarn across from one section to another. Fasten off colors at end of each color section.*

continued on page 97

Captivating displays of enchantment ensnare our imaginations as stars pirouette amongst lofty halos.

Magical Night

by CAROLYN CHRISTMAS

SIZE: 46½" x 61".

MATERIALS: Worsted-weight yarn — 16 oz. teal, 8 oz. each purple and variegated purple/teal; J crochet hook or size needed to obtain gauge.

GAUGE: Rnds 1 and 2 of Large Motif = 4" across. Each Large Motif is 7" across.

SKILL LEVEL: ☆☆ Average

FIRST ROW

First Large Motif

Rnd 1: With purple, ch 4, sl st in first ch to form ring, ch 3, 11 dc in ring, join with sl st in top of ch-3 (12 dc).

Rnd 2: Ch 3, dc in same st, ch 1, (2 dc in next st, ch 1) around, join, fasten off (24 dc, 12 ch-1 sps).

Rnd 3: Join teal with sl st in any ch sp, ch 3, 2 dc in same sp, ch 1, (3 dc in next ch sp, ch 1) around, join (36 dc, 12 ch-1 sps).

Rnd 4: Sl st in next st, ch 3, 4 dc in same st, sc in next ch sp, (5 dc in 2nd dc of next 3-dc group, sc in next ch sp) around, join, fasten off (12 5-dc groups, 12 sc).

Rnd 5: Join variegated with sc in any sc, ch 3, sc in 3rd dc of next 5-dc group, ch 3, (sc in next sc, ch 3, sc in 3rd dc of next 5-dc group, ch 3) around, join with sl st in first sc, fasten off (24 ch-3 sps).

Second Large Motif

Rnds 1-4: Repeat same rnds of First Large Motif.

Rnd 5: Join variegated with sc in any sc; joining to center 4 ch sps on one side of last Motif, ch 1, sl st in first ch sp on last Motif, ch 1, sc in 3rd dc of next 5-dc group on this Motif, ch 1, sl st in next ch sp on other Motif, ch 1, sc in next sc on this Motif, ch 1, sl st in next ch sp on other Motif, ch 1, sc in 3rd dc of next 5-dc group on this Motif, ch 1, sl st in next ch sp on other Motif, ch 1, (sc in next sc on this Motif, ch 3, sc in 3rd dc of next 5-dc group, ch 3) around, join with sl st in first sc, fasten off.

Repeat Second Large Motif 4 more times for a total of 6 Motifs in this row.

SECOND ROW

First Large Motif

Rnds 1-4: Repeat same rnds of First Motif on First Row.

Rnd 5: Join variegated with sc in any sc; joining to bottom of First Large Motif on last row, ch 1, skip next 2 unjoined ch sps on other Motif, sl st in next ch sp, ch 1, sc in 3rd dc of next 5-dc group

continued on next page

Magical Night

Continued from page 95

on this Motif, ch 1, sl st in next ch sp on other Motif, ch 1, sc in next sc on this Motif, ch 1, sl st in next ch sp on other Motif, ch 1, sc in 3rd dc of next 5-dc group on this Motif, ch 1, sl st in next ch sp on other Motif, ch 1, (sc in next sc on this Motif, ch 3, sc in 3rd dc of next 5-dc group, ch 3) around, join with sl st in first sc, fasten off.

Second Motif

Rnds 1-4: Repeat same rnds of First Motif on First Row.

Rnd 5: Join variegated with sc in any sc; joining to bottom of next Motif on last row, *ch 1, skip next 2 unjoined ch sps on other Motif, sl st in next ch sp, ch 1, sc in 3rd dc of next 5-dc group on this Motif, ch 1, sl st in next ch sp on other Motif, ch 1, sc in next sc on this Motif, ch 1, sl st in next ch sp on other Motif, ch 1, sc in 3rd dc of next 5-dc group on this Motif, ch 1, sl st in next ch sp on other Motif, ch 1*, sc in next sc on this Motif, ch 3, sc in 3rd dc of next 5-dc group, ch 3, sc in next sc on this Motif; joining to side of last Motif on this row; repeat between **, (sc in next sc on this Motif, ch 3, sc in 3rd dc of next 5-dc group, ch 3) around, join with sl st in first sc, fasten off.

Repeat Second Large Motif 4 more times for a total of 6 Motifs on this row.

Repeat Second Row 6 more times for a total of 8 rows.

FILLER MOTIF

Rnd 1: With variegated, ch 4, sl st in first ch to form ring, ch 3, 11 dc in ring, join with sl st in top of ch-3 (12 dc).

Rnd 2: Ch 1, sc in first st, ch 2; joining to Large Motifs, sl st in first joined ch sp between any 2 Large Motifs, ch 2, sc in same st on this Motif, *[ch 2, sl st in next joined ch sp between Large Motifs, ch 2, sc in next st on this Motif], (ch 1, sl st in next ch-3 sp on Large Motif, ch 1, sc in next st on this Motif) 2 times, ch 2, sl st in next joined ch sp between Large Motifs, ch 2, sc in same st on this Motif; repeat from * 2 more times; repeat between [ ], ch 1, sl st in next ch-3 sp on Large Motif, ch 1, sc in next st on this Motif, ch 1, sl st in next ch-3 sp on Large Motif, ch 1, join with sl st in first sc on

this Motif, fasten off.

Work Filler Motif in space between each joined Large Motif.

BORDER

*NOTE: For **shell**, (3 dc, ch 1, 3 dc) in next st.*

Rnd 1: Join variegated with sc in first sc after joining ch sp between any Large Motifs, (shell in next sc, sc in next sc) across this Motif, ch 1, *sc in next sc on next Motif, (shell in next sc, sc in next sc) across this Motif, ch 1; repeat from * around, join with sl st in first sc.

*NOTE: For **picot**, ch 2, sl st in 2nd ch from hook.*

Rnd 2: Sl st in each of next 3 sts, sl st in next ch sp, ch 1, (sc, picot, sc) in same sp, *ch 3, sc in next sc, ch 3, (sc, picot, sc) in next ch sp*; repeat between ** across to next ch sp between Large Motifs, ch 1, skip next ch sp between Large Motifs, [(sc, picot, sc) in next ch sp on next Large Motif; repeat between ** across to next ch sp between Large Motifs, ch 1, skip next ch sp between Large Motifs]; repeat between [ ] around, join, fasten off.◆

Fall Prisms

Continued from page 92

HALF DOUBLE CROCHET/ COLOR CHANGE

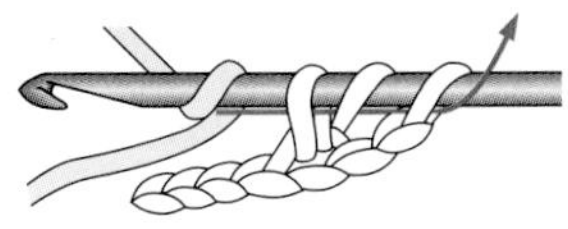

Row 1: With green, ch 21, hdc in 3rd ch from hook, hdc in each ch across, turn (20).

Rows 2-6: Ch 2, hdc in each st across, turn. At end of last row, change to white in last st made.

Row 7: For **row 7 of graph,** ch 2, hdc in next 5 sts changing to lt. colored scrap yarn in last st made, hdc in next st changing to dk. colored scrap yarn, hdc in next 6 sts changing to lt. colored scrap yarn in last st made, hdc in next st changing to white, hdc in last 6 sts, turn.

Rows 8-32: Ch 2, hdc in each st across changing colors according to graph, turn.

Rows 33-182: Repeat rows 7-32 consecutively, ending with row 26.

Row 183: Join green with sl st in first st, ch 2, hdc in each st across, turn.

Rows 184-188: Ch 2, hdc in each st across, turn. At end of last row, fasten off.

Holding Strips wrong sides together, matching ends of rows, working through both thicknesses, with Side Strips on outside edges and alternating Prism and Center Strips, with green, sew Strips together.

EDGING

Rnd 1: Working around entire outer edge, join lt. yellow with sl st in any st, ch 2, hdc in each st and in end of each row around with (hdc, ch 1, hdc) in each corner st, join with sl st in top of ch-2.

Rnd 2: Ch 1, sc in each st and in each ch around, join with sl st in first sc, fasten off.◆

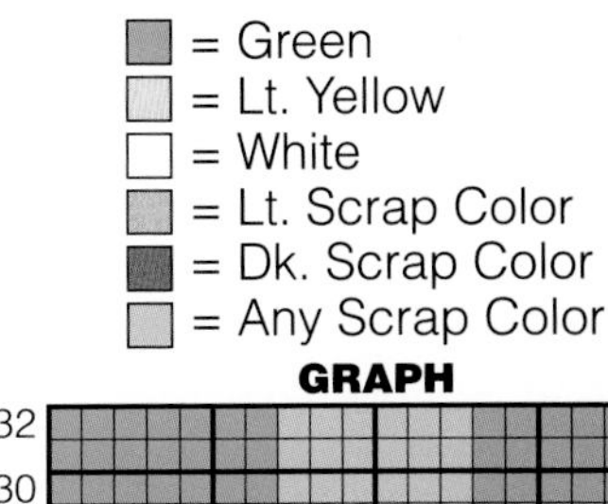

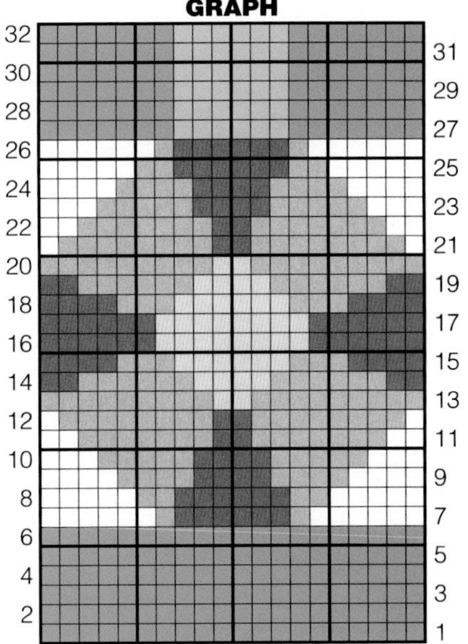

Each square on graph = 1 hdc.

Working on my crafting, as quiet as can be, sitting here a' stitching, just my mommy and me.

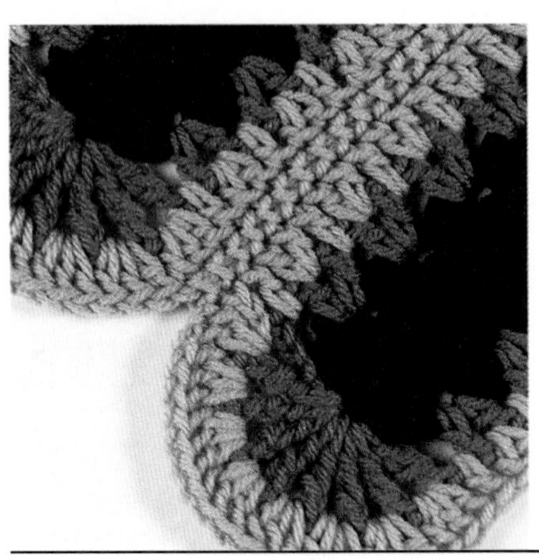

Grape Jelly

by CHRISTINE GRAZIOSO

SIZE: 47" x 65½".

MATERIALS: Worsted-weight yarn — 18 oz. dk. plum, 15 oz. lt. plum and 11 oz. pale plum; tapestry needle; I crochet hook or size needed to obtain gauge.

GAUGE: 3 sts = 1"; 4 dc rows and 3 sc rows = 3¾". Strip Center is 1⅞" wide.

SKILL LEVEL: ☆☆ Average

STRIP (make 11)

Center

Row 1: With dk. plum, ch 5, dc in 5th ch from hook, (ch 1, dc in same ch) 3 times, turn (5 dc, 4 ch-1 sps).

Row 2: Ch 4, skip next ch sp, (sc in next ch sp, ch 1) 2 times, dc in 3rd ch of last ch-4, turn (3 ch-1 sps, 2 dc, 2 sc).

Row 3: Ch 1, sc in first st, skip next ch sp, dc in next ch sp, (ch 1, dc in same sp) 2 times, sc in 3rd ch of last ch-4, turn (3 dc, 2 ch sps, 2 sc).

Row 4: Ch 4, (sc in next ch sp, ch 1) 2 times, dc in last st, turn (3 ch-1 sps, 2 dc, 2 sc).

Rows 5-115: Repeat rows 3 and 4 alternately, ending with row 3. At end of last row, **do not** turn, fasten off.

Border

Rnd 1: Join lt. plum with sl st in base of starting ch, ch 5, tr in same ch, (ch 1, tr in same ch) 7 times; [working in ends of rows, skip first row, *(dc, ch 1, dc) in next row, skip next row; repeat from * across], tr in center dc of last row, (ch 1, tr in same st) 8 times; repeat between [ ], join with sl st in 4th ch of ch-5, fasten off (130 ch-1 sps).

Rnd 2: Join pale plum with sl st in first ch sp, ch 3, 2 dc in same sp, 3 dc in each of next 7 ch sps, *dc in sp between next 2 sts, (2 dc in next ch sp, dc in sp between next 2 sts) 57 times*, 3 dc in each of next 8 ch sps; repeat between **, join with sl st in top of ch-3, fasten off.

Holding Strips wrong sides together, matching sts, with pale plum, leaving six 3-dc groups on each end unworked, sew long edges together.◆

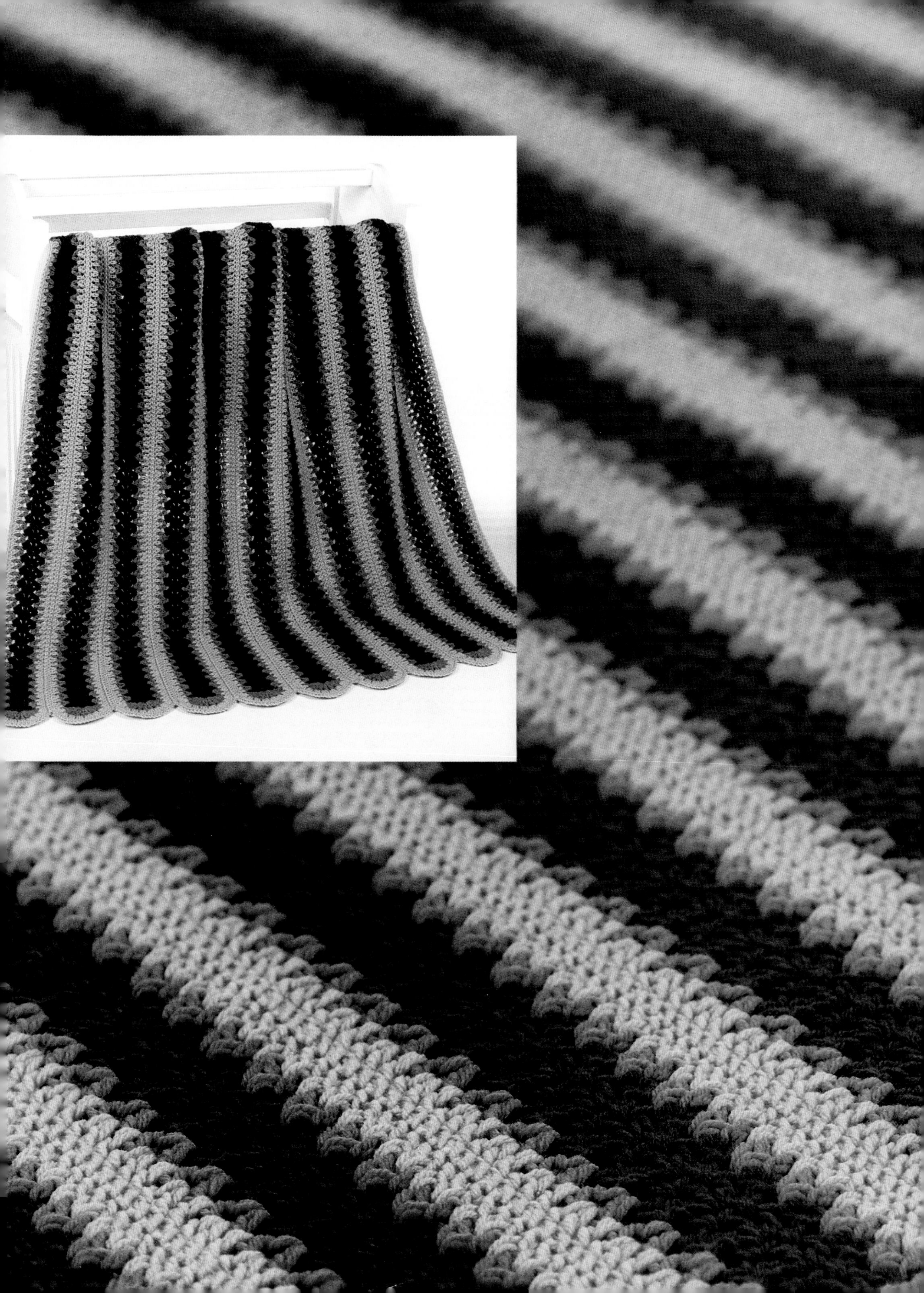

Shadows strolling through the night, reaching toward the dawn, softly scattered by the light, in minutes they'll be gone.

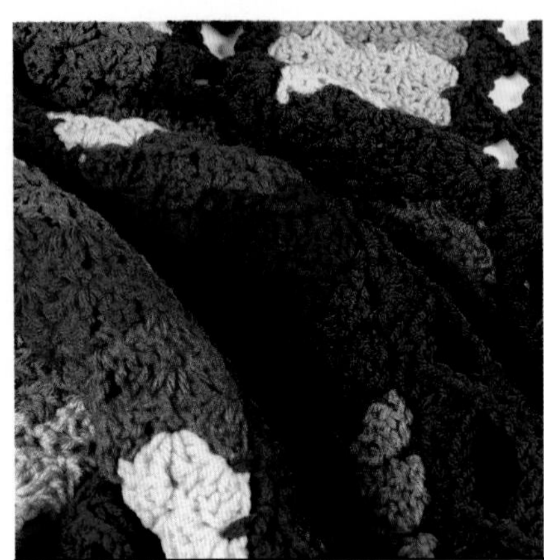

Moonlit Lane

by KATHERINE ENG

SIZE: 46" x 61½".

MATERIALS: Worsted-weight yarn — 25 oz. assorted scrap colors and 14 oz. navy; tapestry needle; I crochet hook or size needed to obtain gauge.

GAUGE: 3 sc and 2 shells = 3¾"; 4 shell rows and 4 sc rows = 4¼".

SKILL LEVEL: ☆☆ Average

FIRST PANEL

Row 1: With any scrap color, ch 14, sc in 2nd ch from hook, sc in each ch across, turn (13 sc).

Row 2: Ch 1, sc in first st, (ch 3, skip next 2 sts, sc in next st) 4 times, turn (5 sc, 4 ch-2 sps).

*NOTES: For **shell,** (2 dc, ch 2, 2 dc) in next st.*

*For **beginning half shell (beg half shell),** ch 3, 2 dc in same st.*

*For **ending half shell (end half shell),** 3 dc in last st.*

Row 3: Ch 1, sc in first sc, (shell in next sc, sc in next sc) across, turn (3 sc, 2 shells).

Row 4: Beg half shell, sc in ch sp of next shell, shell in next sc, sc in ch sp of next shell, 3 dc in last st, turn (2 sc, 2 half shells, 1 shell).

Row 5: Ch 1, sc in first st, shell in next sc, sc in next shell, shell in next sc, sc in last st, turn (3 sc, 2 shells).

Row 6: Repeat row 4, fasten off.

Rnd 7: Join next scrap color with sc in first st, shell in next sc, sc in next shell, shell in next sc, sc in last st, turn.

Rows 8-10: Repeat rows 4 and 5 alternately, ending with row 4. At end of last row, fasten off.

Rows 11-106: Repeat rows 7-10 consecutively. At end of last row, **do not** fasten off.

Row 107: Ch 1, sc in each of first 2 sts, hdc in next st, dc in next st, hdc in next st, sc in next st, sl st in next ch sp, sc in next st, hdc in next st, dc in next st, hdc in next st, sc in each of last 2 sts, turn (13 sts).

Row 108: Ch 1, sc in each st across, turn, fasten off.

Edging

Rnd 1: Working around outer edge in sts and in ends of rows, join navy with sc in last st on last row, ch 2, sc in same st, ch 1, skip first sc row, sc in next sc row, (ch 3, skip next dc row, sc in next sc row) 52 times, ch 3, skip next sc row, sc in next sc row, ch 1; working in starting ch on opposite side of row 1, (sc, ch 2, sc) in first ch, ch 1, skip next ch, (sc in next ch, ch 2, skip next 2 chs, sc in next ch, ch 1, skip next ch) 2 times, (sc, ch 2, sc) in last ch, ch 1, sc in first sc row, ch 3, skip next sc row, sc in

continued on page 107

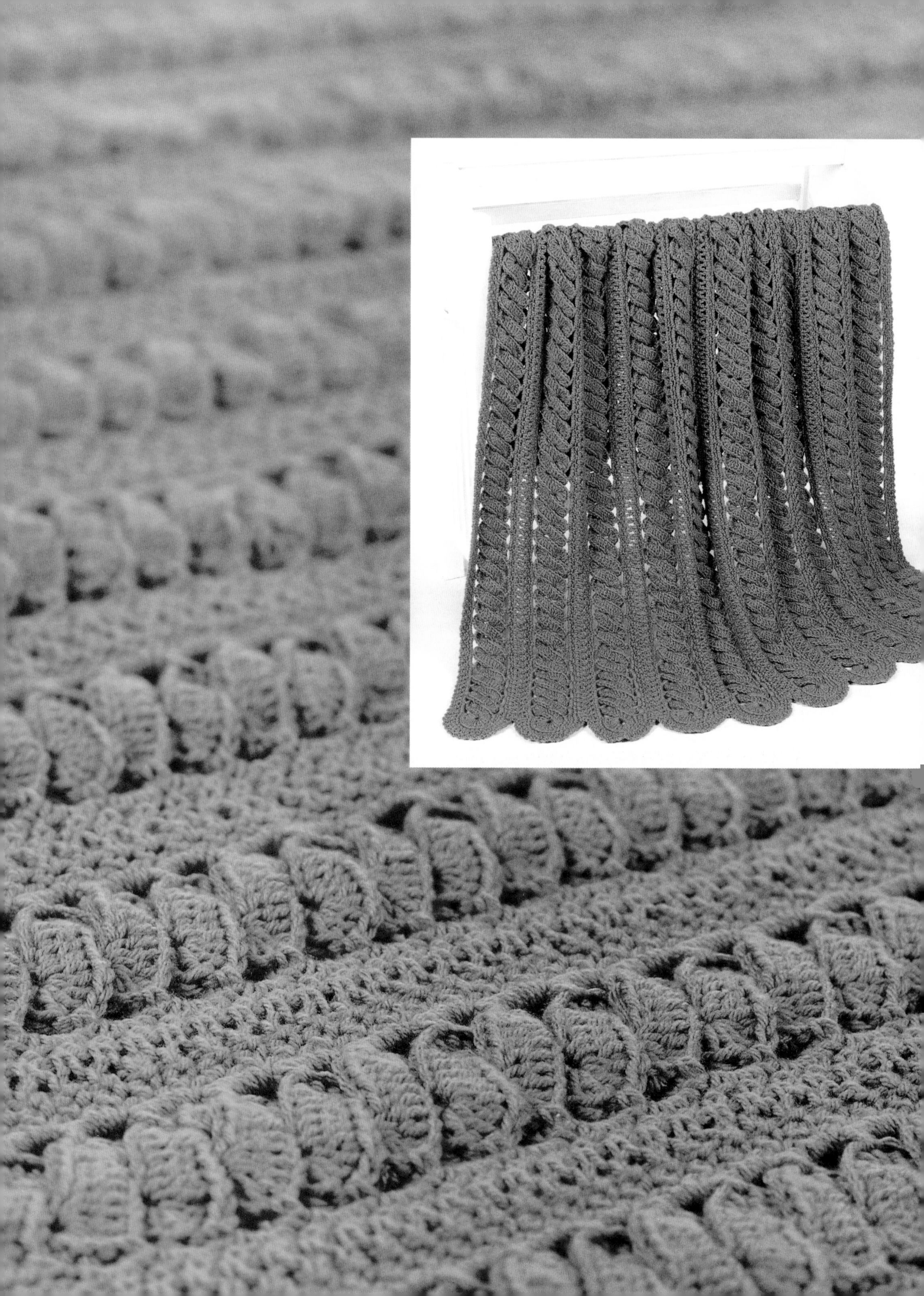

Easier than it looks, this masterpiece of intertwinement will add a new twist to your collection and hone those creative skills.

Braided Sage

by DIANA SIPPEL

SIZE: 49" x 56".

MATERIALS: Worsted-weight yarn — 56 oz. green; tapestry needle; H crochet hook or size needed to obtain gauge.

GAUGE: 7 sts = 2"; 3 twists = 3¾".

SKILL LEVEL: ☆☆ Average

PANEL (make 10)

NOTE: *For* ***decrease (dec),*** *(yo, insert hook in next ch, yo, draw lp through, yo, draw through 2 lps on hook) 8 times, yo, draw through all 9 lps on hook.*

Rnd 1: Ch 601, 7 dc in 4th ch from hook; for **first side,** *dc in each of next 2 chs, dec, dc in each of next 2 chs, (8 dc in next ch, dc in each of next 2 chs, dec, dc in each of next 2 chs) 22 times*, 16 dc in next ch; for **second side,** repeat between **, twist curves over and under each other according to Twist Diagram on page 108, 8 dc in same ch as first st, join with sl st in top of ch-3 (23 decs and 22 8-dc groups across each long edge between 16-dc groups).

Rnd 2: Ch 1, sc in first st, 2 sc in next st, (sc in next st, 2 sc in next st) 2 times, *ch 4, sc in 5th ch at base of next dec, ch 4, (sc in 5th dc of next 8-dc group, ch 4, sc in 5th ch at base of next dec, ch 4) across to 16-dc group on next end, skip next 2 sts*, (sc in next st, 2 sc in next st) 6 times; repeat between **, (sc in next st, 2 sc in next st) 3 times, join with sl st in first sc (46 ch-4 sps across each side between 18 sc on each end).

Rnd 3: Ch 1; working in **back lps** only, sc in first 9 sts; 4 sc in each ch sp across to next end; working in **back lps** only, sc in next 18 sts; 4 sc in each ch sp across to first end; working in **back lps** only, sc in last 9 sts, join.

Rnd 4: Ch 1, sc in first st, (ch 1, sc in next st) 8 times, *ch 1, skip next st, (sc in next st, ch 1, skip next st) 92 times*, sc in next st, (ch 1, sc in next st) 16 times; repeat between **, (sc in next st, ch 1) 8 times, join, fasten off.

To **join Panels,** holding 2 Panels side by side, join with sc in 9th ch sp on first Panel, ch 3, sc in corresponding ch sp on 2nd Panel, ch 3, sl st in next ch sp on first Panel, (ch 3, sl st in next ch sp on 2nd Panel, ch 3, sl st in next ch sp on first Panel) 92 times, fasten off.

Join remaining Panels in same manner.

EDGING

Join with sl st in first ch-1 sp after any joining ch-3 sp, (ch 1, sl st in next ch-1 sp) across to next joining ch-3 sp, 2 dc in next joining ch-3 sp, *sl st

continued on page 108

Display grand eloquence with a colonial appeal, as laced centers softly define joined-as-you-go borders.

Pinwheel Lace

by MAGGIE WELDON

SIZE: 49½ " x 72½".

MATERIALS: Worsted-weight yarn — 24 oz. each white and sage; I crochet hook or size needed to obtain gauge.

GAUGE: Rnds 1-3 of Motif = 4½". Each Motif is 8" across.

SKILL LEVEL: ☆☆ Average

FIRST MOTIF

Rnd 1: With white, ch 3, sl st in first ch to form ring, ch 1, sc in ring, (ch 5, sc in ring) 5 times; to **join,** ch 2, dc in first sc (6 ch-5 sps).

Rnd 2: Ch 1, sc around joining dc, ch 5, (sc in next ch sp, ch 5) around, join with sl st in first sc.

Rnd 3: Sl st in next ch sp, ch 3, (5 dc, 2 tr, ch 4, sc) in same sp, (6 dc, 2 tr, ch 4, sc) in next 4 ch sps, (6 dc, 3 tr) in last ch sp, **do not** join (54 sts, 5 ch-4 sps).

Rnd 4: Ch 5, skip next 2 sts, *(sc in next st, ch 5, skip next 2 sts) 2 times, sc in top of ch-4, ch 5, skip next 3 sts; repeat from * 4 more times, sc in next st, ch 5, skip next 2 sts, sc in next st; to **join,** ch 2, skip next 2 sts, dc in last st (18 ch sps).

Rnd 5: Ch 1, sc around joining dc, ch 6, (sc in next ch sp, ch 6) around, join with sl st in first sc, fasten off.

Rnd 6: Join sage with sl st in any ch sp, ch 3, (2 dc, ch 2, 3 dc) in same sp, 3 dc in next ch sp, 2 dc in next ch sp, *(3 dc, ch 2, 3 dc) in next ch sp, 3 dc in next ch sp, 2 dc in next ch sp; repeat from * around, join with sl st in top of ch-3 (66 dc, 6 ch-2 sps).

Rnd 7: Sl st in next st, ch 1, sc in same st, ch 3, skip next st, (sc, ch 3, sc) in next ch sp, *ch 3, skip next st, (sc in next st, ch 3, skip next st) 5 times, (sc, ch 3, sc) in next ch sp; repeat from * 4 more times, ch 3, skip next st, (sc in next st, ch 3, skip next st) 4 times, join with sl st in first sc, fasten off (42 ch-3 sps).

ONE-SIDE JOINED MOTIF

Rnds 1-6: Repeat same rnds of First Motif.

Rnd 7: Sl st in next st, ch 1, sc in same st, ch 3, skip next st; joining to next Motif (see Joining Diagram on page 106), sc in next ch sp, ch 1, sl st in 2nd ch of corresponding ch sp on other Motif, ch 1, sc in same sp on this Motif, ch 1, sl st in 2nd ch of next ch-3 sp on other Motif, ch 1, skip next st on this Motif, (sc in next st, ch 1, sl st in 2nd ch of next ch-3 sp on other Motif, ch 1, skip next st on this Motif) 5 times, sc in next ch sp, ch 1, sl st in 2nd ch of next ch-3 sp on other Motif, ch 1, sc in same sp on this Motif, *ch 3, skip next st, (sc in

continued on page 106

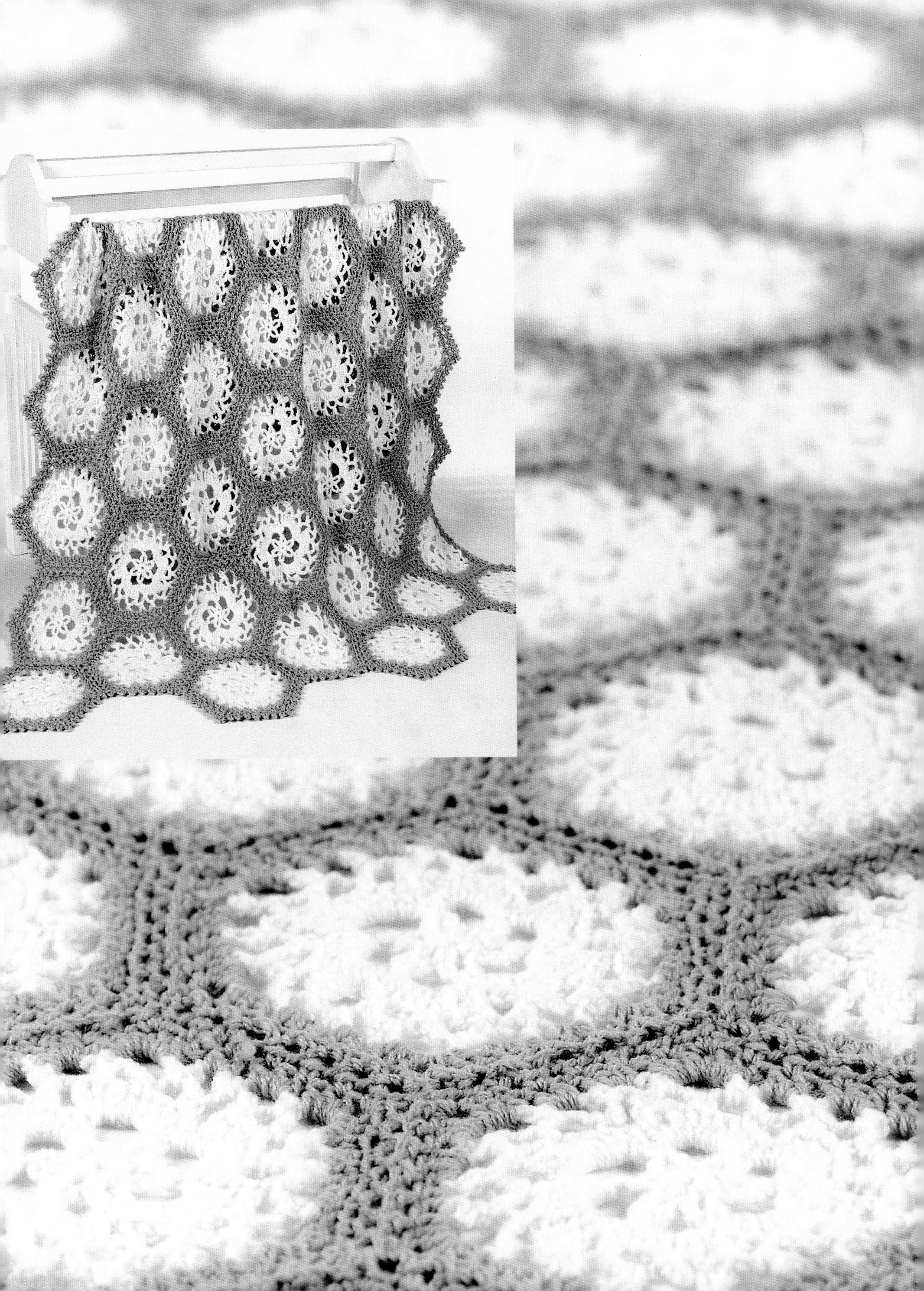

Pinwheel Lace

Continued from page 104

next st, ch 3, skip next st) 5 times, (sc, ch 3, sc) in next ch sp; repeat from * 3 more times, ch 3, skip next st, (sc in next st, ch 3, skip next st) 4 times, join with sl st in first sc, fasten off.

2-SIDE JOINED MOTIF

Rnds 1-6: Repeat same rnds of First Motif on page 104.

Rnd 7: Sl st in next st, ch 1, sc in same st, ch 3, skip next st; joining to next Motif (see diagram), sc in next ch sp, ch 1, sl st in 2nd ch of corresponding ch sp on other Motif, ch 1, sc in same sp on this Motif, *ch 1, sl st in 2nd ch of next ch-3 sp on other Motif, ch 1, skip next st on this Motif, (sc in next st, ch 1, sl st in 2nd ch of next ch-3 sp on other Motif, ch 1, skip next st on this Motif) 5 times*, sc in next ch sp, ch 1, sl st in joining sl st between Motifs, ch 1, sc in same sp on this Motif; joining to next Motif; repeat between **, sc in next ch sp, ch 1, sl st in 2nd ch of next ch sp on other Motif, ch 1, sc in same sp on this Motif, [ch 3, skip next st, (sc in next st, ch 3, skip next st) 5 times, (sc, ch 3, sc) in next ch sp]; repeat between [ ] 2 more times, ch 3, skip next st, (sc in next st, ch 3, skip next st) 4 times, join with sl st in first sc, fasten off.

3-SIDE JOINED MOTIF

Rnds 1-6: Repeat same rnds of First Motif.

Rnd 7: Sl st in next st, ch 1, sc in same st, ch 3, skip next st; joining to next Motif (see diagram), sc in next ch sp, ch 1, sl st in 2nd ch of corresponding ch sp on other Motif, ch 1, sc in same sp on this Motif, *[ch 1, sl st in 2nd ch of next ch-3 sp on other Motif, ch 1, skip next st on this Motif, (sc in next st, ch 1, sl st in 2nd ch of next ch-3 sp on other Motif, ch 1, skip next st on this Motif) 5 times], sc in next ch sp, ch 1, sl st in joining sl st between Motifs, ch 1, sc in same sp on this Motif*; joining to next Motif, repeat between **; joining to next Motif; repeat between [ ], sc in next ch sp, ch 1, sl st in 2nd ch of next ch sp on other Motif, ch 1, sc in same sp on this Motif, ◊ch 3, skip next st, (sc in next st, ch 3, skip next st) 5 times, (sc, ch 3, sc) in next ch sp; repeat from◊, ch 3, skip next st, (sc in next st, ch 3, skip next st) 4 times, join with sl st in first sc, fasten off.

Work and join Motifs according to Joining Diagram.

JOINING DIAGRAM

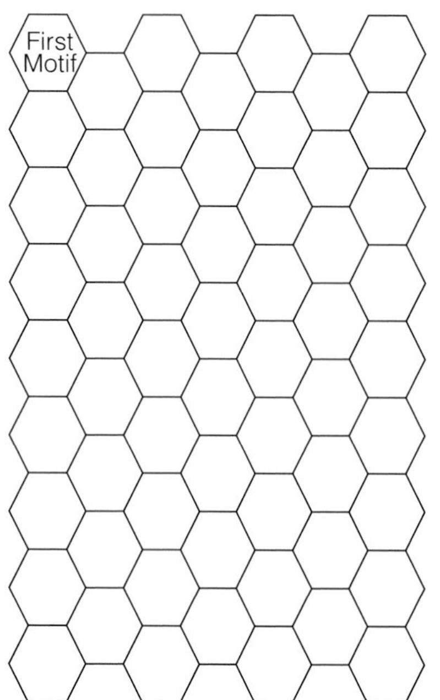

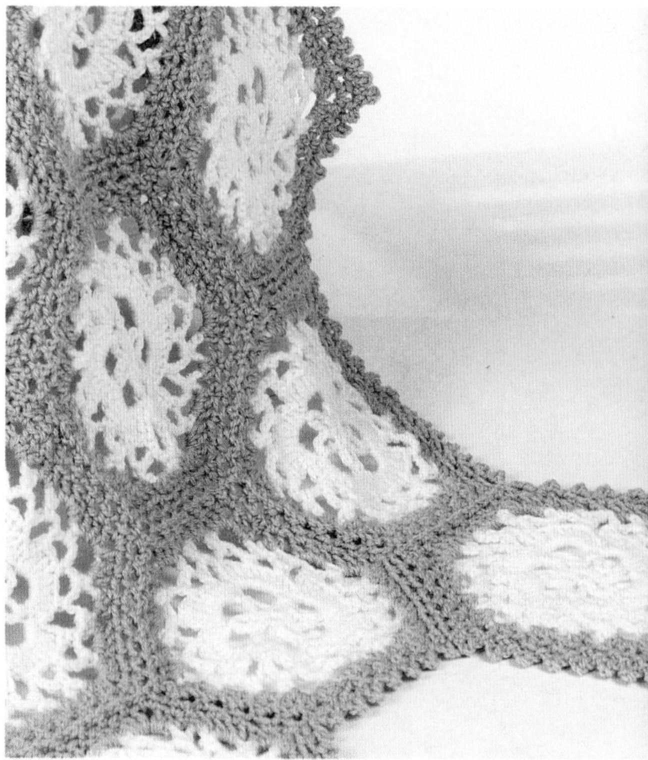

EDGING

***NOTE:** For **picot,** ch 4, sl st in 3rd ch from hook, ch 1.*

Join sage with sl st in any corner ch sp, picot, sl st in same sp, picot; skipping each joined ch sp before and after joining sl sts, (sl st in next ch sp or joining sl st between Motifs, picot) across to next corner ch sp, *(sl st, picot, sl st) in next corner ch sp, picot, (sl st in next ch sp or joining sl st between Motifs, picot) across to next corner ch sp; repeat from * around, join with sl st in first sl st, fasten off.◆

Moonlit Lane

Continued from page 100

next sc row, (ch 3, skip next dc row, sc in next sc row) 52 times, ch 1, skip last sc row, (sc, ch 2, sc) in first st, ch 1, skip next st, (sc in next st, ch 2, skip next 2 sts, sc in next st, ch 1, skip next st) 2 times, join with sl st in first sc (5 ch sps across each short end between corner ch sps, 55 ch sps across each long edge between corner ch sps).

*NOTE: For **beginning shell (beg shell)**, ch 3, (dc, ch 2, 2 dc) in same sp.*

Rnd 2: Sl st in next ch sp, beg shell, (sc, ch 2, sc) in next ch sp, *shell in next ch sp, (sc, ch 2, sc) in next ch sp; repeat from * around, join with sl st in top of ch-3, fasten off.

SECOND PANEL

Work same as First Panel on page 100.

Edging

Rnd 1: Repeat same rnd of First Panel Edging on page 100.

*NOTES: For **joining shell**, 2 dc in next ch sp, ch 1, drop lp from hook, insert hook in ch sp of corresponding shell on other Panel, draw dropped lp through, ch 1, 2 dc in same sp on this Panel.*

Every other Panel will be upside down after joining.

Rnd 2: Sl st in next ch sp, beg shell, (sc, ch 2, sc) in next ch sp, *shell in next ch sp, (sc, ch 2, sc) in next ch sp; repeat from * 29 more times; joining to right long edge of last Panel, work joining shell, [(sc, ch 2, sc) in next ch sp, work joining shell]; repeat between [ ] 27 more times, (sc, ch 2, sc) in next ch sp, ◊shell in next ch sp, (sc, ch 2, sc) in next ch sp; repeat from ◊, join with sl st in top of ch-3, fasten off.

THIRD PANEL

Work same as First Panel.

Edging

Rnd 1: Repeat same rnd of First Panel Edging.

*NOTE: For **beginning joining shell (beg joining shell)**, ch 3, dc in same sp, ch 1, drop lp from hook, insert hook in ch sp of corresponding shell on other Panel, draw dropped lp through, ch 1, 2 dc in same sp on this Panel.*

Rnd 2: Sl st in next ch sp; joining to unjoined long edge of last Panel, work beg joining shell, *(sc, ch 2, sc) in next ch sp, work joining shell; repeat from * 27 more times, (sc, ch 2, sc) in next ch sp, [shell in next ch sp, (sc, ch 2, sc) in next ch sp]; repeat between [ ] around, join with sl st in top of ch-3, fasten off.

Repeat Second and Third Panels alternately for a total of 7 Panels.

BORDER

Rnd 1: Working around entire outer edge, join navy with sl st in corner ch sp before one short end, ch 3, (2 tr, ch 2, 2 tr, dc) in same sp, [ch 1, dc in next ch sp, ch 1, (shell in next shell, ch 1, dc in next ch sp, ch 1) 2 times, *dc in next joined ch sp, (2 tr, ch 2, 2 tr) around next joining st, dc in next joined ch sp, ch 1, dc in next ch sp, ch 1, (shell in next shell, ch 1, dc in next ch sp, ch 1) 2 times; repeat from * across to next corner ch sp, (dc, 2 tr, ch 2, 2 tr, dc) in next corner ch sp, ch 1, dc in next ch sp, ch 1, (shell in next shell, ch 1, dc in next ch sp, ch 1) across] to next corner ch sp, (dc, 2 tr, ch 2, 2 tr, dc) in next corner ch sp; repeat between [ ], join with sl st in top of ch-3.

Rnd 2: Sl st in each of next 2 sts, sl st in next corner ch sp, ch 1, (sc, ch 2, sc, ch 3, sc, ch 2, sc) in same sp; work this rnd in the following Steps:

Step A: ch 3, [◊(sc in next ch sp, ch 2) 2 times, *(sc, ch 2, sc) in next shell, (ch 2, sc in next ch sp) 2 times*, ch 2; repeat between **◊, ch 3, (sc, ch 3, sc) in next ch sp, ch 3]; repeat between [ ] 5 more times; repeat between ◊◊, ch 3;

Step B: (sc, ch 2, sc, ch 3, sc, ch 2, sc) in next corner ch sp, ch 3, sc in next ch sp, ch 2, sc in next ch sp, *ch 2, (sc, ch 2, sc) in next shell, (ch 2, sc in next ch sp) 2 times; repeat from * across to next corner ch sp, ch 3;

Step C: (sc, ch 2, sc, ch 2, sc, ch 2, sc) in next corner ch sp, repeat Step A;

Step D: repeat step B, join with sl st in first sc, fasten off.◆

Braided Sage

Continued from page 103

in next ch-1 sp, (ch 1, sl st in next ch-1 sp) across to next joining ch-3 sp, 2 dc in next joining ch-3 sp; repeat from * around, join with sl st in first sl st, fasten off.◆

TWIST DIAGRAM

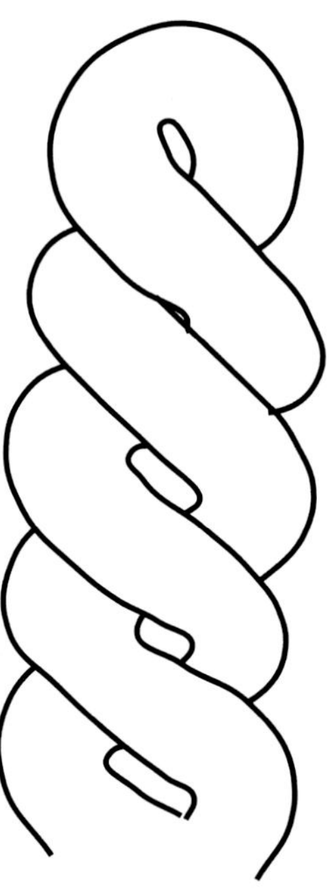

Butterscotch & Caramel

Continued from page 91

Holding Panels right sides together, matching sts, with gold, sew long edges together through **back bars** of sts (see illustration).

BACK BAR OF HDC

EDGING

Rnd 1: With wrong side of work facing you, join gold with sc in any corner ch sp, (tr, sc) in same sp; *[working in sts and seams, tr in next st, (sc in next st or seam, tr in next st) across] to next corner ch sp, (sc, tr, sc) in next corner ch sp; repeat from * 2 more times; repeat between [ ], join with sl st in first sc, **turn.**

Rnd 2: Ch 1, sc in each st around with (sc, ch 2, sc) in each corner tr, join, fasten off.◆

Harvest, Bounty & Family

Chapter Six

Afghan Splendor

Geometric symmetry prevails throughout as classic granny square and rectangular strewn pathways enticingly lead the way.

Forest Path

by MARGRET WILLSON

SIZE: 53" x 73".

MATERIALS: Worsted-weight yarn — 38 oz. green, 29 oz. variegated and 12 oz. honey; tapestry needle; H crochet hook or size needed to obtain gauge.

GAUGE: 7 sts = 2". Each Square is 3¼" across. Each Rectangle is 3¼" x 6½".

SKILL LEVEL: ☆☆ Average

SQUARE (make 84 variegated and 42 honey)

NOTES: *For* ***beginning cluster (beg cl),*** *ch 3, (yo, insert hook in same sp, yo, draw lp through, yo, draw through 2 lps on hook) 3 times, yo, draw through all 4 lps on hook.*

For ***cluster (cl),*** *yo, insert hook in next ch sp, yo, draw lp through, yo, draw through 2 lps on hook, (yo, insert hook in same sp, yo, draw lp through, yo, draw through 2 lps on hook) 3 times, yo, draw through all 5 lps on hook.*

Rnd 1: Ch 4, sl st in first ch to form ring, ch 4, (dc in ring, ch 1) 7 times, join with sl st in 3rd ch of ch-4 (8 dc, 8 ch-1 sps).

Rnd 2: Sl st in next ch sp, beg cl, ch 3, (cl in next ch sp, ch 3) around, join with sl st in top of beg cl.

Rnd 3: Sl st in next ch sp, ch 3, (2 dc, ch 3, 3 dc) in same sp, 3 dc in next ch sp, *(3 dc, ch 3, 3 dc) in next ch sp, 3 dc in next ch sp; repeat from * around, join with sl st in top of ch-3, fasten off (36 dc, 4 ch-3 sps).

RECTANGLE (make 84)

Row 1: With green, ch 4, dc in 4th ch from hook, **turn,** (ch 3, dc in 3rd ch from hook, **turn)** 3 times, ch 3, dc in 3rd ch from hook, **do not** turn (5 lps across each side).

Rnd 2: Working in rnds, ch 3, 2 dc in first ch lp, 3 dc in each of next 3 ch lps, (3 dc, ch 3, 3 dc, ch 3, 3 dc) in last ch lp; working across opposite side of ch lps, 3 dc in each of next 3 ch lps, (3 dc, ch 3, 3 dc, ch 3) in same ch lp as first st, join with sl st in top of ch-3, **turn** (12 3-dc groups, 4 ch-3 sps).

Rnd 3: Sl st in next corner ch sp, ch 1, (sc, ch 3, sc) in same sp, *ch 3, (sc, ch 3, sc) in next corner ch sp, ch 3, (sc in sp between next 2 3-dc groups, ch 3) 4 times*, (sc, ch 3, sc) in next corner ch sp; repeat between **, join with sl st in first sc, **turn** (16 ch-3 sps).

Rnd 4: Sl st in next corner ch sp, ch 3, 2 dc in same sp, 3 dc in each of next 4 ch sps, *(3 dc, ch 3, 3 dc) in next corner ch sp, 3 dc in next ch sp, (3 dc, ch 3, 3 dc) in next corner ch sp*, 3 dc in each of next 5 ch sps; repeat between **, join with sl st in top of ch-3, fasten off (60 dc, 4 ch-3 sps).

Holding Squares and Rectangles wrong sides

continued on page 117

Lovingly crocheted with leftover yarn and simple stitches, these dangling strands of heartfelt messages seem suspended in air.

String of Hearts

by MAGGIE WELDON

SIZE: 45" x 58½".

MATERIALS: Worsted-weight yarn — 35 oz. natural, 21 oz. assorted scrap colors and 4 oz. lt. brown; tapestry needle; H crochet hook or size needed to obtain gauge.

GAUGE: 7 sc = 2"; 7 sc rows = 2". Each Strip is 7¼" wide.

SKILL LEVEL: ☆☆ Average

STRIP (make 6)

Row 1: With natural, ch 20, sc in 2nd ch from hook, sc in each ch across, turn (19 sc).

Row 2: Ch 1, sc in each st across, turn.

***NOTES:** Front of row 1 is right side of work.*

When changing colors (see page 159), always drop color to wrong side of work. Use a separate ball of yarn for each color section. ***Do not*** *carry yarn across from one section to another. Fasten off colors at end of each color section.*

Work odd-numbered rows of graph from right to left and even-numbered rows from left to right.

Each square on graph equals one sc.

Row 3: For **row 3 of graph** (see page 117), ch 1, sc in first 9 sts changing to any scrap color in last st made, sc in next st changing to natural, sc in last 9 sts, turn.

Rows 4-18: Ch 1, sc in each st across changing colors according to graph, turn.

Rows 19-194: Repeat rows 3-18 consecutively.

Rows 195-196: Ch 1 , sc in each st across, turn.

Rnd 197: Working around outer edge, ch 1, 3 sc in first st, sc in each st and in end of each row around with 3 sc in each corner st, join with sl st in first sc.

Rnd 198: Ch 3, dc in each st around with (2 dc, ch 2, 2 dc) in each center corner st, join with sl st in top of ch-3, fasten off.

Holding Strips wrong sides together, matching sts, with natural, sew long edges together through **back lps.**

EDGING

Working around entire outer edge, join natural with sl st in any corner ch sp, ch 3, (dc, ch 2, 2 dc) in same sp, dc in each st and 2 dc in each ch sp on each side of seams around with (2 dc, ch 2, 2 dc) in each corner ch sp, join with sl st in top of ch-3, fasten off.◆

graph on page 117

Envision a handmade treasure that's sure to please even the most discriminating tastes as this variety of thickly textured front and back post stitches undulate across in neutral colors.

Tawny Ripples

by DIANE POELLOT

SIZE: 53" x 62".

MATERIALS: Worsted-weight yarn — 51 oz. off-white, 30 oz. cream and 18 oz. beige; tapestry needle; G crochet hook or size needed to obtain gauge.

GAUGE: 4 sts = 1"; 7 pattern rows = 3½". Each Panel is 7" wide.

SKILL LEVEL: ☆☆☆ Advanced

PANEL (make 7)

Row 1: With off-white, ch 232, sc in 2nd ch from hook, (hdc in next ch, dc in next ch, tr in next ch, skip next ch, 3 tr in next ch, skip next ch, tr in next ch, dc in next ch, hdc in next ch, sc in next ch) across, turn (231 sts).

NOTES: *For* ***double crochet front post (dc fp),*** *yo, insert hook from front to back around post of next st, yo, draw lp through, (yo, draw through 2 lps on hook) 2 times.*

For ***treble crochet front post (tr fp),*** *yo 2 times, insert hook from front to back around post of next st, yo, draw lp through, (yo, draw through 2 lps on hook) 3 times.*

For ***dc fp decrease (dc fp dec),*** **yo, insert hook from front to back around post of next st, yo, draw lp through, yo, draw through 2 lps on hook*, skip next st; repeat between **, yo, draw through all 3 lps on hook.*

Row 2: Ch 1, sc in first st, ch 1, dc fp around each of next 4 sts, dc in next st, tr fp around same st, dc in same st, (dc fp around each of next 3 sts, dc fp dec, dc fp around each of next 3 sts, dc in next st, tr fp around same st, dc in same st) across to last 5 sts, dc fp around each of next 4 sts leaving last st unworked, **do not** turn, fasten off. Front of row 2 is right side of work.

NOTES: *First sc and next ch-1 sp is not used or counted as a st.*

For ***tr fp decrease (tr fp dec),*** **yo, insert hook from front to back around post of next st, yo, draw lp through, yo, draw through 2 lps on hook*, yo 2 times, insert hook from front to back around post of skipped st on row before last, yo, draw lp through, (yo, draw through 2 lps on hook) 2 times, skip next dec on last row; repeat between **, yo, draw through all 4 lps on hook.*

For ***dc fp last 2 sts tog,*** *(yo, insert hook from front to back around post of next st, yo, draw lp through, yo, draw through 2 lps on hook) 2 times, yo, draw through all 3 lps on hook.*

Row 3: Join cream with sc in first dc fp, ch 1, dc fp around each of next 4 sts, dc in next st, tr fp around same st, dc in same st, (dc fp around each of next 3 sts, tr fp dec, dc fp around each of next

continued on next page

Tawny Ripples

Continued from page 115

3 sts, dc in next st, tr fp around same st, dc in same st) across to last 5 sts, dc fp around each of next 3 sts, dc fp last 2 sts tog, **do not** turn, fasten off.

NOTE: *For* ***tr fp dec on remaining rows,*** **yo, insert hook from front to back around post of next dc fp, yo, draw lp through, yo, draw through 2 lps on hook*, yo 2 times, insert hook from front to back around post of center st on next tr dec, yo, draw lp through, (yo, draw through 2 lps on hook) 2 times; repeat between **, yo, draw through all 4 lps on hook.*

Row 4: With beige, repeat row 3.

Row 5: With cream, repeat row 3.

Row 6: With off-white, repeat row 3, **turn, do not** fasten off.

NOTES: *For* ***single crochet back post (sc bp),*** *insert hook from back to front around post of next st, yo, draw lp through, yo, draw through both lps on hook.*

For ***half double crochet back post (hdc bp),*** *yo, insert hook from back to front around post of next st, yo, draw lp through, yo, draw through all 3 lps on hook.*

For ***double crochet back post (dc bp),*** *yo, insert hook from back to front around post of next st, yo, draw lp through, (yo, draw through 2 lps on hook) 2 times.*

For ***treble crochet back post (tr bp),*** *yo 2 times, insert hook from back to front around post of next st, yo, draw lp through, (yo, draw through 2 lps on hook) 3 times.*

Beginning ch-3 and next tr bp on next row counts as tr bp first 2 sts tog.

Row 7: Ch 3, tr bp around each of next 2 sts, dc bp around next st, hdc bp around next st, sc bp around next st, hdc bp around next st, dc bp around next st, tr bp around next st, [*yo 2 times, insert hook from back to front around post of next dc fp, yo, draw lp through, (yo, draw through 2 lps on hook) 2 times*, yo 2 times, insert hook from back to front around post of center st on next tr dec, yo, draw lp through, (yo, draw through 2 lps on hook) 2 times; repeat between **, yo, draw through all 4 lps on hook, tr bp around next st, dc bp around next st, hdc bp around next st, sc bp around next st, hdc bp around next st, dc bp around next st, tr bp around next st]; repeat between [ ] across to last 2 sts, tr bp last 2 sts tog, **do not** turn, fasten off (185 sts).

Row 8: Working in starting ch on opposite side of row 1, join off-white with sc in first ch, (hdc in next ch, dc in next ch, tr in next ch, skip next ch, 3 tr in next ch, skip next ch, tr in next ch, dc in next ch, hdc in next ch, sc in next ch) across, turn (231 sts).

Rows 9-14: Repeat rows 2-7.

Holding Panels right sides together, matching sts, with off-white, sl st Panels together through **front lps.**

BORDER

Rnd 1: Working around entire outer edge, with right side of work facing you, join off-white with sl st in first st on one long edge, ch 4, 2 tr in same st, ◊(tr in next st, dc in next st, hdc in next st, sc in next st, hdc in next st, dc in next st, tr in next st, 3 tr in next st) across; working in ends of rows, (tr, dc) in first row, *[(hdc, sc, hdc) in next row, (dc, tr) in next row, 3 tr in next row, tr in next row, dc in next row, hdc in next row, sc in end of starting ch, hdc in next row, dc in next row, tr in next row, 3 tr in next row, (tr, dc) in next row, (hdc, sc, hdc) in next row, (dc, tr) in next row], 3 tr in seam, (tr, dc) in next row; repeat from * 5 more times; repeat between [ ]◊; working in sts across long edge, 3 tr in first st; repeat between ◊◊, join with sl st in top of ch-4 (209 sts across each short end between corner tr, 229 sts across each long edge between corner tr).

NOTE: *First sc fp and ch-2 counts as dc fp.*

Rnd 2: Ch 1, sc fp around first st, ch 2, dc in same st, *[dc in next center corner st, tr fp around same st, dc in same st, dc in next st, dc fp around same st, dc fp around each of next 2 sts, dc fp dec, (dc fp around each of next 3 sts, dc in next st, tr fp around same st, dc in same st, dc fp around each of next 3 sts, dc fp dec) across to 3 sts before next center corner tr, dc fp around each of next 2 sts], dc fp around next st, dc in same st; repeat from * 2 more times; repeat between [ ], join with sl st in top of ch-2, fasten off.

Rnd 3: Join cream with sc fp around first st, ch 2, dc fp around each of next 2 sts, *[dc in next center corner st, tr fp around same st, dc in same st, dc fp around next 4 sts, tr fp dec, (dc fp around each of next 3 sts, dc in next st, tr fp around same st, dc in same st, dc fp around each of next 3 sts, tr fp dec) across] to 4 sts before next center corner st, dc fp around next 4 sts; repeat from * 2 more times; repeat between [ ] across to last st, dc fp around last st, join, fasten off.

Rnd 4: Join beige with sc fp around first st, ch 2, dc fp around each of next 3 sts, *[dc in next center corner st, tr fp around same st, dc in same st, dc fp around next 4 sts, tr fp dec, (dc fp around each of next 3 sts, dc in next st, tr fp around same st, dc in same st, dc fp around each of next 3 sts, tr fp dec)] across to 4 sts before next center corner tr, dc fp around next 4 sts; repeat from * 2 more times; repeat between [ ], join, fasten off.◆

Forest Path

Continued from page 110

together, matching sts, sew together through **back lps** according to Assembly Diagram.

EDGING

Working around entire outer edge, with one strand variegated and honey held together, join with sc in any st, sc in each st and in each ch sp on each side of seams around with (2 sc, ch 2, 2 sc) in each corner ch sp, join with sl st in first sc, fasten off.◆

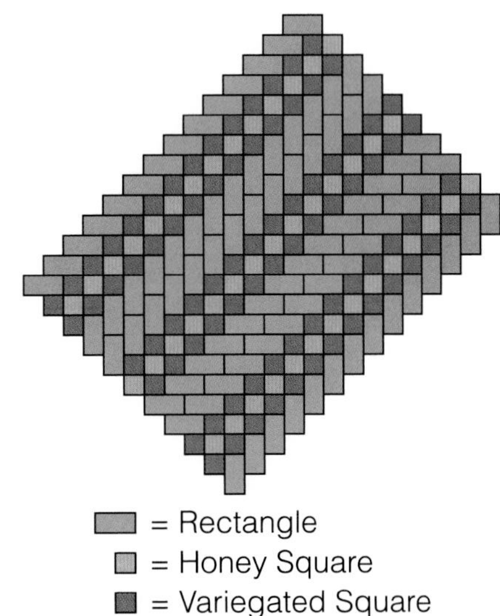

String of Hearts

Instructions on page 113

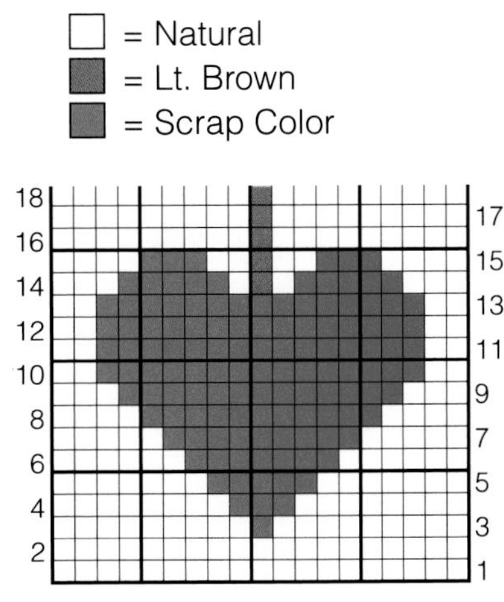

Each square on graph = 1 sc.

Easy to make on the go or at home, these white clusters bloom abundantly in diamond shaped motifs, sewn together and trimmed with tassels.

Impressions

by MAGGIE WELDON

SIZE: 58" x 74" not including Tassels.

MATERIALS: Worsted-weight yarn — 24 oz. each white and med. aqua and 18 oz. dk. aqua; tapestry needle; I crochet hook or size needed to obtain gauge.

GAUGE: Rnd 1 of Motif = 2½" across. Each Motif is 6" square.

SKILL LEVEL: ☆☆ Average

MOTIF (make 111)

*NOTES: For **beginning cluster (beg cl),** ch 4, *yo 2 times, insert hook in ring, yo, draw lp through, (yo, draw through 2 lps on hook) 2 times; repeat from *, yo, draw through all 3 lps on hook.*

*For **cluster (cl),** *yo 2 times, insert hook in ring, yo, draw lp through, (yo, draw through 2 lps on hook) 2 times; repeat from * 2 more times, yo, draw through all 4 lps on hook.*

Rnd 1: With white, ch 4, sl st in first ch to form ring, beg cl, ch 3, (cl, ch 3) 7 times in ring, join with sl st in top of beg cl, fasten off (8 cls, 8 ch-3 sps).

Rnd 2: Join dk. aqua with sc in any ch sp, 4 sc in same sp, 5 sc in each ch sp around, join with sl st in first sc, fasten off (40 sc).

Rnd 3: Join med. aqua with sc in center sc of any 5-sc group, sc in same st, *[ch 1, (3 dc, ch 2, 3 dc) in center sc of next 5-dc group, ch 1], 2 sc in center sc of next 5-sc group; repeat from * 2 more times; repeat between [ ], join (32 sts, 8 ch-1 sps, 4 ch-2 sps).

Rnd 4: Ch 3, dc in each st and in each ch around with (2 dc, ch 2, 2 dc) in each corner ch-2 sp, join with sl st in top of ch-3, fasten off (56 dc, 4 ch-2 sps).

Rnd 5: Join dk. aqua with sc in any corner ch sp, 2 sc in same sp, sc in each st around with 3 sc in each corner ch sp, join with sl st in first sc, fasten off.

Matching sts, with dk. aqua, sew Motifs together through **back lps** according to Assembly Diagram.

TASSEL (make 14)

Cut 30 strands white each 12" long. Tie separate strand white tightly around middle of all strands; fold strands in half. Wrap another strand white around folded strands 1" from top of fold covering ½"; secure and hide ends inside Tassel. Trim all ends evenly.

Tie one Tassel to each point on each short end of Afghan.◆

ASSEMBLY DIAGRAM

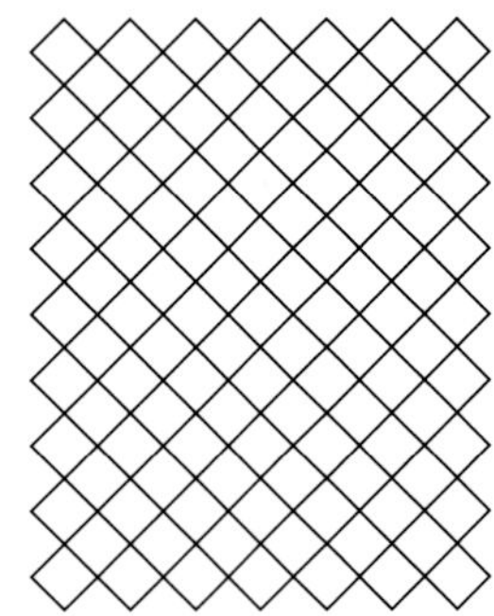

A yield of fall colors in festive ripples worked across strips of granny squares, celebrate hearty feelings of thanksgiving.

Indian Harvest

by MARGRET WILLSON

SIZE: 58" x 74".

MATERIALS: Worsted-weight yarn — 30 oz. aran, 12 oz. each green and camel, 8 oz. each autumn ombre (ombre) and rust; H crochet hook or size needed to obtain gauge.

GAUGE: Four 3-dc groups = 3"; 4 dc rows and 4 sc rows worked in pattern = 3". Rnds 1-3 of Motif = 3" across. Each Motif is 4½" square.

SKILL LEVEL: ☆☆☆ Advanced

STRIP A (make 3)

First Motif

Rnd 1: With rust, ch 4, sl st in first ch to form ring, ch 3, 15 dc in ring, join with sl st in top of ch-3, **turn** (16 dc).

Rnd 2: Ch 1, sc in first st, ch 3, skip next st, (sc in next st, ch 3, skip next st) around, join with sl st in first sc, **turn,** fasten off (8 ch-3 sps).

*NOTES: For **beginning popcorn (beg pc),** ch 3, 3 dc in same sp, drop lp from hook, insert hook in top of ch-3, draw dropped lp through.*

*For **popcorn (pc),** 4 dc in next ch sp, drop lp from hook, insert hook in first dc of 4-dc group, draw dropped lp through.*

Rnd 3: Join variegated with sl st in any ch sp, beg pc, ch 3, pc in same sp, ch 1, pc in next ch sp, ch 1, *(pc, ch 3, pc) in next ch sp, ch 1, pc in next ch sp, ch 1; repeat from * around, join with sl st in top of beg pc, **do not** turn, fasten off (8 ch-1 sps, 4 ch-3 sps).

Rnd 4: Join camel with sl st in any corner ch-3 sp, ch 3, (2 dc, ch 3, 3 dc) in same sp, 3 dc in each of next 2 ch-1 sps, *(3 dc, ch 3, 3 dc) in next corner ch-3 sp, 3 dc in each of next 2 ch-1 sps; repeat from * around, join with sl st in top of ch-3, fasten off (16 3-dc groups, 4 ch-3 sps).

Rnd 5: Join green with sc in any corner ch sp, ch 3, sc in same sp, ch 3, (sc in sp between next two 3-dc groups, ch 3) 3 times, *(sc, ch 3, sc) in next corner ch sp, ch 3, (sc in sp between next two 3-dc groups, ch 3) 3 times; repeat from * around, join with sl st in first sc, fasten off (20 ch-3 sps).

Second Motif

Rnds 1-4: Repeat same rnds of First Motif.

Rnd 5: Join green with sc in any corner ch sp; joining to corner ch sp on end of last Motif, ch 1, sc in corner ch sp on other Motif, ch 1, sc in same sp on this Motif, ch 3, (sc in sp between next two 3-dc groups, ch 3) 3 times, *(sc, ch 3, sc) in next corner ch sp, ch 3, (sc in sp between next two 3-dc groups, ch 3) 3 times; repeat from * around,

continued on next page

Indian Harvest

Continued from page 121

join with sl st in first sc, fasten off.

Repeat Second Motif 7 more times for a total of 9 Motifs.

STRIP B (make 2)

First Half Motif

Row 1: With rust, ch 4, sl st in first ch to form ring, ch 3, 7 dc in ring, turn (8 dc).

Row 2: Ch 1, sc in first st, ch 3, sc in next st, (ch 3, skip next st, sc in next st, ch 3, sc in next st) 2 times, turn, fasten off (5 ch-3 sps).

Row 3: Join ombre with sl st in first st, ch 4, (pc in next ch sp, ch 1) 2 times, (pc, ch 3, pc) in next ch sp, ch 1, (pc in next ch sp, ch 1) 2 times, dc in last st, **do not** turn, fasten off (6 ch-1 sps, 1 ch-3 sp).

Row 4: Join camel with sl st in 3rd ch of ch-4, ch 3, 3 dc in each of next 3 ch-1 sps, (3 dc, ch 3, 3 dc) in next ch-3 sp, 3 dc in each of next 3 ch-1 sps, dc in last st, **do not** turn, fasten off (8 3-dc groups, 2 dc, 1 ch-3 sp).

Row 5: Join green with sc in sp between first st and next 3-dc group, ch 3, sc in same sp, ch 3, (sc in sp between next two 3-dc groups, ch 3) 3 times, (sc, ch 3, sc) in next ch sp, ch 3, (sc in sp between next two 3-dc groups, ch 3) 3 times, (sc, ch 3, sc) in sp between last 3-dc group and last dc, fasten off (11 ch-3 sps).

Second Motif

Rnds 1-4: Repeat same rnds of Strip A First Motif on page 121.

Rnd 5: Joining to ch-3 sp on center point of First Half Motif, repeat same rnd of Strip A Second Motif on page 121.

Third Motif

Work same as Strip A Second Motif.

Repeat Third Motif 6 more times for a total of 9 Motifs.

Last Half Motif

Rows 1-4: Repeat same rows of First Half Motif.

Row 5: Join green with sc in sp between first st and next 3-dc group, ch 3, sc in same sp, ch 3, (sc in sp between next two 3-dc groups, ch 3) 3 times, sc in next ch sp; joining to last Motif, ch 1, sc in corner ch sp on end of other Motif, ch 1, sc in same sp on this Motif, ch 3, (sc in sp between next two 3-dc groups, ch 3) 3 times, (sc, ch 3, sc) in sp between last 3-dc group and last dc, fasten off.

FIRST SIDE

First Ripple Section

Row 1: Working across one side of one Strip A, with wrong side facing you, join green with sc in first corner ch sp on end of Strip, ch 3, (sc in next ch sp, ch 3) 4 times, (sc, ch 3, sc) in next corner ch sp, ch 3, (sc in next ch sp, ch 3) 4 times, *sc in next joining sc, ch 3, skip joined ch sp, (sc in next ch sp, ch 3) 4 times, (sc, ch 3, sc) in next corner ch sp, ch 3, (sc in next ch sp, ch 3) 4 times; repeat from * 7 more times, sc in end ch sp, turn, fasten off (99 ch-3 sps).

*NOTES: For **cluster (cl)**, yo, insert hook in next ch sp, yo, draw lp through, yo, draw through 2 lps on hook, yo, insert hook in same sp, yo, draw lp through, yo, draw through 2 lps on hook, yo, draw through all 3 lps on hook.*

*For **5-dc decrease (5-dc dec)**, *yo, insert hook in next ch-3 sp, yo, draw lp through, yo, draw through 2 lps on hook, yo, insert hook in same sp, yo, draw lp through, yo, draw through 2 lps on hook*, yo, insert hook in next sc or in next ch-1 sp, yo, draw lp through, yo, draw through 2 lps on hook; repeat between **, yo, draw through all 6 lps on hook.*

Row 2: Join aran with sl st in first st, ch 3, cl in next ch sp, 3 dc in each of next 4 ch sps, (3 dc, ch 3, 3 dc) in next ch sp, 3 dc in each of next 4 ch sps, *5-dc dec, 3 dc in each of next 4 ch sps, (3 dc, ch 3, 3 dc) in next ch sp, 3 dc in each of next 4 ch sps; repeat from * across to last ch sp, cl in next ch sp, dc in last st, turn.

Row 3: Ch 1, sc in first st, sc in sp between next cl and next 3-dc group, *[ch 3, (sc in sp between next two 3-dc groups, ch 3) 4 times, (sc, ch 3, sc) in next ch sp, ch 3, (sc in sp between next two 3-dc groups, ch 3) 4 times], sc in sp between next 3-dc group and next 5-dc dec, ch 1, sc in sp between same 5-dc dec and next 3-dc group; repeat from * 7 more times; repeat between [ ], sc in sp between same 3-dc group and next cl, sc in last st, turn (99 ch-3 sps, 8 ch-1 sps).

Row 4: Ch 3, cl in next ch sp, 3 dc in each of next 4 ch sps, (3 dc, ch 3, 3 dc) in next ch sp, 3 dc in each of next 4 ch sps, *5-dc dec, 3 dc in each of next 4 ch sps, (3 dc, ch 3, 3 dc) in next ch sp, 3 dc in each of next 4 ch sps; repeat from * across to last ch sp, cl in last ch sp, dc in last st, turn.

Rows 5-6: Repeat rows 3 and 4. At end of last row, fasten off.

Row 7: Join rust with sc in first st, sc in sp between next cl and next 3-dc group, ch 3, *[(sc in sp between next two 3-dc groups, ch 3) 4 times, (sc, ch 3, sc) in next ch sp, ch 3, (sc in sp between next two 3-dc groups, ch 3) 4 times], sc in sp between next 3-dc group and next 5-dc dec, ch 1, sc in sp between same 5-dc dec and next 3-dc group, ch 3; repeat from * 7 more times; repeat between [ ], sc in sp between next 3-dc group and next cl, sc in last st, turn, fasten off.

Rows 8-10: Repeat rows 2-4. At end of last row, fasten off.

Row 11: With green, repeat row 7.

Rows 12-14: Repeat rows 2-4. At end of last row, fasten off.

Row 15: Repeat row 7.

Row 16: Repeat row 2.

Rows 17-20: Repeat rows 3 and 4 alternately. At end of last row, fasten off.

Row 21: Join green with sc in first st, sc in sp between next cl and next 3-dc group, joining to one side of one Strip B, ch 1, sc in first ch sp on Strip B, ch 1, *[(sc in sp between next two 3-dc groups on this Section, ch 1, sl st in next ch sp on Strip B, ch 1) 4 times, (sc in next ch sp on this Section, ch 1, sc in joining sc on Strip B, ch 1, sc in same sp on this Section, ch 1, sc in next ch sp on Strip B, ch 1, (sc in sp between next two 3-dc groups on this Section, ch 1, sc in next ch sp on Strip B, ch 1) 4 times], sc in sp between next 3-dc group and next 5-dc dec on this Section, ch 1, sc in sp between same 5-dc dec and next 3-dc group, ch 1, sc in next ch sp on Strip B, ch 1; repeat from * 7 more times; repeat between [ ], sc in sp between next 3-dc group and next cl on this Section, sc in last st, fasten off.

Second Ripple Section

Row 1: Working across opposite side of same joined Strip B, with wrong side facing you, join green with sc in first ch sp on end of Strip B, ch 3, (sc in next ch sp, ch 3) 4 times, *[sc in joining sc, ch 3, skip joined ch sp, (sc in next ch sp, ch 3) 4 times], (sc, ch 3, sc) in next corner ch sp, ch 3, (sc in next ch sp, ch 3) 4 times; repeat from * 7 more times; repeat between [ ], sc in last ch sp, turn, fasten off (98 ch-3 sps).

Row 2: Join aran with sl st in first st, ch 3, dc in same st, *[3 dc in each of next 4 ch sps, 5-dc dec, 3 dc in each of next 4 ch sps], (3 dc, ch 3, 3 dc) in next ch sp; repeat from * 7 more times; repeat between [ ], 2 dc in last st, turn.

Row 3: Ch 1, sc in first st, ch 3, sc in sp between next dc and next 3-dc group, ch 3, (sc in sp between next two 3-dc groups, ch 3) 3 times, *[sc in sp between next 3-dc group and next 5-dc dec, ch 1, sc in sp between same 5-dc dec and next 3-dc group, ch 3], (sc in sp between next two 3-dc groups, ch 3) 4 times, (sc, ch 3, sc) in next ch sp, ch 3, (sc in sp between next two 3-dc groups, ch 3) 4 times; repeat from * 7 more times; repeat between [ ], (sc in sp between next two 3-dc groups, ch 3) 3 times, sc in sp between next 3-dc group and next dc, ch 3, sc in last dc, turn (98 ch-3 sps, 9 ch-1 sps).

Row 4: Ch 3, dc in same st, *[3 dc in each of next 4 ch sps, 5-dc dec, 3 dc in each of next 4 ch sps], (3 dc, ch 3, 3 dc) in next ch sp; repeat from * 7 more times; repeat between [ ], 2 dc in last st, turn.

Rows 5-6: Repeat rows 3 and 4. At end of last row, fasten off.

Row 7: Join rust with sc in first st, ch 3, sc in sp between next dc and next 3-dc group, ch 3, (sc in sp between next two 3-dc groups, ch 3) 3 times, *[sc in sp between next 3-dc group and next 5-dc dec, ch 1, sc in sp between same 5-dc dec and next 3-dc group, ch 3], (sc in sp between next two 3-dc groups, ch 3) 4 times, (sc, ch 3, sc) in next ch sp, ch 3, (sc in sp between next two 3-dc groups, ch 3) 4 times; repeat from * 7 more times; repeat between [ ], (sc in sp between next two 3-dc groups, ch 3) 3 times, sc in sp between next 3-dc group and next dc, ch 3, sc in last dc, turn, fasten off.

Rows 8-10: Repeat rows 2-4. At end of last row, fasten off.

Row 11: With green, repeat row 7.

Rows 12-14: Repeat rows 2-4. At end of last row, fasten off.

Row 15: Repeat row 7.

Row 16: Repeat row 2.

Rows 17-20: Repeat rows 3 and 4 alternately. At end of last row, fasten off.

Row 21: Join green with sc in first st; joining to long edge of another Strip A, ch 1, sc in first ch sp on Strip A, ch 1, sc in sp between next dc and next 3-dc group on this Section, ch 1, sc in next ch sp on Strip A, ch 1, (sc in sp between next two 3-dc groups on this Section, ch 1, sc in next ch sp on Strip A, ch 1) 3 times, *[sc in sp between next 3-dc group and next 5-dc dec on this Section, ch 1, sc in sp between same 5-dc dec and next 3-dc group, ch 1, sc in same sp on Strip A, ch 1], (sc in sp between next two 3-dc groups on this Section, ch 1, sc in next ch sp on Strip A, ch 1) 4 times, sc in next ch sp, ch 1, sc in next joining sc on Strip A, ch 1, sc in same sp on this Section, ch 1, sc in next ch sp on Strip A, ch 1, (sc in sp between next two 3-dc groups, ch 1, sc in next ch sp on Strip A, ch 1) 4 times; repeat from * 7 more times; repeat between [ ], (sc in sp between next two 3-dc groups on this Section, ch 1, sc in next ch sp on Strip A, ch 1) 3 times, sc in sp between next 3-dc group and next dc on this Section, ch 1, sc in last ch sp on Strip A, ch 1, sc in last dc on this Section, fasten off.

Third Ripple Section

Rows 1-6: Working across opposite side of same joined Strip A, repeat same rows of First Ripple Section.

SECOND SIDE

Working across opposite side of first Strip A,

continued on page 127

Two-tones of luscious color and airy spaces of openwork lend a lacy effect beckoning fragrant memories of summer.

Country Garden

by CAROLYN CHRISTMAS

SIZE: 50" x 63½" not including Fringe.

MATERIALS: Worsted-weight yarn — 16 oz. lt. green, 10 oz. med. green, 8 oz. lt. rose and 6 oz. each med. rose and aran; I crochet hook or size needed to obtain gauge.

GAUGE: Rnds 1-3 of Motif = 3½" across. Each Motif is 7" across.

SKILL LEVEL: ☆☆ Average

FIRST ROW

First Large Motif

Rnd 1: With med. rose, ch 5, sl st in first ch to form ring, ch 1, (sc, hdc, 2 dc, hdc, sc) 6 times in ring, join with sl st in first sc, fasten off (6 petals).

Rnd 2: Join lt. rose with sl st in **back bar** (see illustration) of any sc, ch 4, (sl st in **back bar** of next sc, ch 4) around, join with sl st in first sl st (6 ch-4 sps).

Rnd 3: Sl st in next ch sp, ch 1, (sc, hdc, 3 dc, hdc, sc) in same sp and in each ch sp around, join with sl st in first sc.

Rnd 4: Working behind petals, ch 4, (sc in sp between next 2 petals, ch 4) around, join with sl st in joining sl st of last rnd, fasten off.

Rnd 5: Join med. green with sl st in any ch sp, ch 3, (2 dc, ch 2, 3 dc) in same sp, ch 1, *(3 dc, ch 2, 3 dc) in next ch sp, ch 1; repeat from * around, join with sl st in top of ch-3, fasten off (36 dc, 6 ch-2 sps, 6 ch-1 sps).

Rnd 6: Join aran with sl st in any ch-2 sp, ch 6, dc in same sp, *[ch 1, skip next st, dc in next st, ch 1, skip next st, dc in next ch-1 sp, ch 1, skip next st, dc in next st, ch 1, skip next st], (dc, ch 3, dc) in next ch-2 sp; repeat from * 4 more times; repeat between [ ], join with sl st in 3rd ch of ch-6, fasten off (24 ch-1 sps, 6 ch-3 sps).

Rnd 7: Join lt. green with sl st in any ch-3 sp, ch 5, hdc in same sp, *[ch 1, (hdc in next ch-1 sp, ch 1) 4 times], (hdc, ch 3, hdc) in next ch-3 sp; repeat from * 4 more times; repeat between [ ], join with sl st in 2nd ch of ch-5, fasten off (30 ch-1 sps, 6 ch-3 sps).

Second Large Motif

Rnds 1-6: Repeat same rnds of First Large Motif.

Rnd 7: Join lt. green with sl st in any ch-3 sp, ch 5, hdc in same sp, ch 1, (hdc in next ch-1 sp, ch 1)

continued on page 126

Country Garden

Continued from page 124

4 times, hdc in next ch-3 sp; joining to bottom of last Motif on this row, ch 1, sl st in corresponding ch-3 sp on other Motif (see Joining Diagram), ch 1, hdc in same sp on this Motif, ch 1, sl st in next ch-1 sp on other Motif, ch 1, (hdc in next ch-1 sp on this Motif, ch 1, sl st in next ch-1 sp on other Motif, ch 1) 4 times, hdc in next ch-3 sp on this Motif, ch 1, sl st in next ch-3 sp on other Motif, ch 1, hdc in same sp on this Motif, *[ch 1, (hdc in next ch-1 sp, ch 1) 4 times], (hdc, ch 3, hdc) in next corner ch-3 sp; repeat from * 2 more times; repeat between [ ], join with sl st in 2nd ch of ch-5, fasten off.

Repeat Second Large Motif 7 more times for a total of 9 Motifs.

SECOND ROW

First Large Motif

Rnds 1-6: Repeat same rnds of First Row First Large Motif on page 124.

Rnd 7: Join lt. green with sl st in any ch-3 sp, ch 5, hdc in same sp, ch 1, (hdc in next ch-1 sp, ch 1) 4 times, hdc in next ch-3 sp; joining to center ch-3 sp on side of First Motif on last row, ch 1, sl st in corresponding ch-3 sp on other Motif (see diagram), ch 1, hdc in same sp on this Motif, *[ch 1, (hdc in next ch-1 sp, ch 1) 4 times], (hdc, ch 3, hdc) in next ch-3 sp; repeat from * 3 more times; repeat between [ ], join with sl st in 2nd ch of ch-5, fasten off.

Second Large Motif

Rnds 1-6: Repeat same rnds of First Row First Large Motif.

Rnd 7: Join lt. green with sl st in any ch-3 sp, ch 5, hdc in same sp, ch 1, (hdc in next ch-1 sp, ch 1) 4 times, hdc in next ch-3 sp; joining to bottom of last Motif on this row, ch 1, sl st in corresponding ch-3 sp on other Motif, ch 1, hdc in same sp on this Motif, ch 1, sl st in next ch-1 sp on other Motif, ch 1, (hdc in next ch-1 sp on this Motif, ch 1, sl st in next ch-1 sp on other Motif, ch 1) 4 times, hdc in next ch-3 sp on this Motif, ch 1, sl st in next ch-3 sp on other Motif, ch 1, hdc in same sp on this Motif, ch 1, (hdc in next ch-1 sp, ch 1) 4 times, hdc in next ch-3 sp, ch 1, sl st in center ch-3 sp on side of next Motif on last row, ch 1, hdc in same sp on this Motif, *[ch 1, (hdc in next ch-1 sp, ch 1) 4 times], (hdc, ch 3, hdc) in next ch-3 sp; repeat from * ; repeat between [ ], join with sl st in 2nd ch of ch-5, fasten off.

Repeat Second Large Motif 7 more times for a total of 9 Motifs.

Repeat Second Row 4 more times for a total of 6 rows.

Filler Motif

Rnd 1: With med. green, ch 4, dc in 4th ch from hook, ch 3, (2 dc in same ch, ch 3) 3 times, join with sl st in top of ch-3, fasten off (8 dc, 4 ch-3 sps).

Rnd 2: Join lt. green with sl st in any ch sp, ch 3, dc in same sp; working in sps between Large Motifs (see diagram), ch 1, sl st in joining sl st between first 2 Motifs on Second row, ch 1, 2 dc in same sp on this Motif, *ch 2, skip next 2 ch-1 sps on other Motif, sl st in next ch sp, ch 2, 2 tr in next ch sp on this Motif, ch 3, sl st in next joining sl st between Motifs, ch 3, 2 tr in same sp on this Motif, ch 2, skip next 2 ch-1 sps on next Motif, sl st in next ch sp, ch 2*, 2 dc in next ch sp on this Motif, ch 1, sl st in next joining sl st between Motifs, ch 1, 2 dc in same sp on this Motif; repeat between **, join, fasten off.

Starting in joining between Large Motifs on right-hand row, repeat Filler Motif in each space between Motifs (see diagram).

Half Motif

Row 1: With med. green, ch 4, (dc, ch 3, 2 dc) in 4th ch from hook, **do not** turn, fasten off (4 dc, 1 ch-3 sp).

Row 2: Join lt. green with sl st in first st, ch 3; joining to First Large Motif on last row, sl st in unworked ch-3 sp before joined ch-3 sp, ch 1, dc in same st on this Motif, ch 2, skip next 2 ch-1 sps on other Motif, sl st in next ch-1 sp, ch 2, 2 tr in next ch sp on this Motif, ch 3, sl st in joining sl st between Large Motifs, ch 3, 2 tr in same sp on this Motif, ch 2, skip next 2 ch-1 sps on next Large Motif, sl st in next ch-1 sp, ch 2, dc in last st on this

Motif, ch 1, sl st in next unworked ch-3 sp on other Motif, dc in same st on this Motif, fasten off.

Repeat Half Motif in each indentation on each short end of Afghan according to diagram.

EDGING

Working around entire outer edge, join lt. green with sc in unjoined ch-3 sp on Large Motif before one long edge as indicated on diagram, (sc, ch 1, 2 sc) in same sp, ◊*[ch 1, hdc in next ch-1 sp, ch 1, (dc in next ch-1 sp, ch 1) 3 times, hdc in next ch-1 sp, ch 1, (2 sc, ch 1, 2 sc) in next ch-3 sp], ch 1, hdc in next ch-1 sp, ch 1, (dc in next ch-1 sp, ch 1) 3 times, hdc in next ch-1 sp, ch 1, sc next 2 joined ch-3 sps tog; repeat from * 7 more times; repeat between [ ] 2 more times, ch 1, (sc, ch 1) in each ch-1 sp, each ch-3 sp and in end of each row or in base of starting ch on each Half Motif across◊ to next unjoined ch-3 sp of last Large Motif on this short end, (2 sc, ch 1, 2 sc) in next ch-3 sp; repeat between ◊◊, join with sl st in first sc, fasten off.

FRINGE

For **each Fringe,** cut 4 strands lt. green each 16" long. With all 4 strands held together, fold in half, insert hook in ch sp, draw fold through, draw all loose ends through fold, tighten. Trim ends.

Fringe in each ch sp on each short end of Afghan.◆

JOINING DIAGRAM

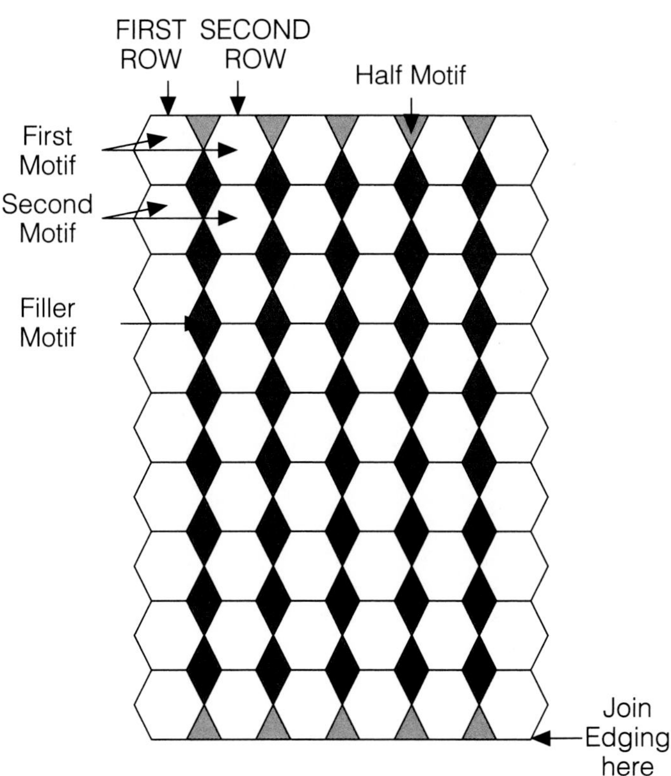

Indian Harvest

Continued from page 123

work same as First Side.

EDGING

Rnd 1: Working around entire outer edge, join camel with sc in any st, sc in each st, 3 sc in each ch sp, sc in end of each sc row and 2 sc in end of each dc row around with 3 sc in each corner, join with sl st in first sc.

Rnd 2: Ch 1, sc in each st around with 3 sc in center st of each 3-sc group, join, fasten off.◆

Acknowledging an end to summer's reign, variegated panels in blends of rust and green, invoke images of a swirling leaf's descent to gently kiss the ground.

Autumn Splendor

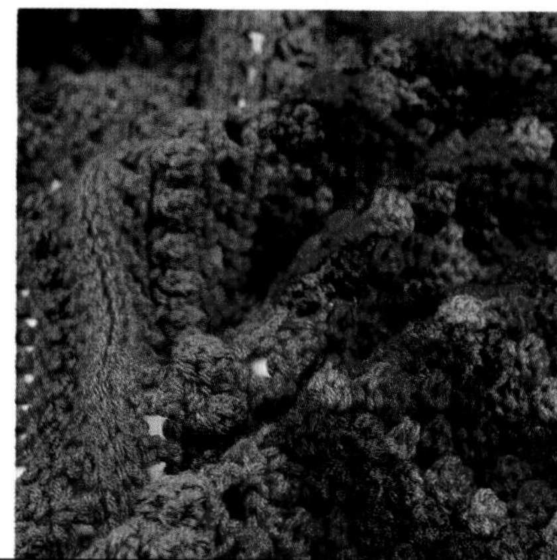

by ELEANOR ALBANO-MILES

SIZE: 43½" x 58".

MATERIALS: Worsted-weight yarn — 29 oz. rust/dk. green variegated, 21 oz. rust and 12 oz. dk. green; tapestry needle; H crochet hook or size needed to obtain gauge.

GAUGE: 7 sts = 2"; 10 sc rows = 3".

SKILL LEVEL: ☆☆ Average

PANEL A (make 2)

Center

Row 1: With variegated, ch 18, sc in 2nd ch from hook, sc in each ch across, turn (17 sc).

Row 2: Ch 1, sc in first st, (tr in next st, sc in next st) across, turn.

Row 3: Ch 1, sc in each st across, turn.

Row 4: Ch 1, sc in each of first 2 sts, tr in next st, (sc in next st, tr in next st) across to last 2 sts, sc in each of last 2 sts, turn.

Row 5: Ch 1, sc in each st across, turn.

Rows 6-163: Repeat rows 2-5 consecutively, ending with row 3. At end of last row, **do not** turn, fasten off.

Edging

Rnd 1: Working around outer edge, join rust with sc in first st on last row, ch 2, sc in same st, sc in each st across to last st, (sc, ch 2, sc) in last st; *working in ends of rows, skip first row, sc in each row across to last row, skip last row*; working in starting ch on opposite side of row 1, (sc, ch 2, sc) in first ch, sc in each ch across to last ch, (sc, ch 2, sc) in last ch; repeat between **, join with sl st in first sc, **turn** (17 sc across each short end between corner ch-2 sps, 163 sc across each long edge between corner ch-2 sps).

Rnd 2: Sl st in next st, ch 4, skip next st, *(dc in next st, ch 1, skip next st) across to next corner ch sp, (dc, ch 2, dc) in next corner ch sp, ch 1, skip next st; repeat from * around, join with sl st in 3rd ch of ch-4, **turn.**

Rnd 3: Ch 1, sc in each st and in each ch-1 sp around with (sc, ch 2, sc) in each corner ch-2 sp, join with sl st in first sc, **turn,** fasten off (21 sc across each short end between corner ch-2 sps, 167 sc across each long edge between corner ch-2 sps).

Rnd 4: Join dk. green with sc in any corner ch sp, ch 2, sc in same sp, *[tr in next st, (sc in next st, tr in next st) across] to next corner ch sp, (sc, ch 2, sc) in next corner ch-2 sp; repeat from * 2 more times; repeat between [ ], join, **turn,** fasten off.

Rnd 5: Join rust with sc in any corner ch sp, sc in each st around with (sc, ch 2, sc) in each corner ch sp, join, **turn.**

continued on next page

Autumn Splendor

Continued from page 129

Rnds 6-7: Repeat rnds 2 and 3, ending with 29 sc across each short end between corner ch sps, 175 sc across each long edge between corner ch sps.

PANEL B (make 2)

Center

Row 1: With variegated, ch 18, sc in 2nd ch from hook, sc in each ch across, turn (17 sc).

*NOTE: For **cluster (cl),** yo, insert hook in next st, yo, draw lp through, yo, draw through 2 lps on hook, (yo, insert hook in same st, yo, draw lp through, yo, draw through 2 lps on hook) 2 times, yo, draw through all 4 lps on hook.*

Row 2: Ch 1, sc in first st, (cl in next st, sc in next st) across, turn.

Row 3: Ch 1, sc in each st across, turn.

Row 4: Ch 1, sc in each of first 2 sts, cl in next st, (sc in next st, cl in next st) across to last 2 sts, sc in each of last 2 sts, turn.

Row 5: Ch 1, sc in each st across, turn.

Rows 6-163: Repeat rows 2-5 consecutively, ending with row 3. At end of last row, **do not** turn, fasten off.

Edging

Rnds 1-3: Repeat same rnds of Panel A Edging on page 129.

Rnd 4: Join dk. green with sc in any corner ch sp, ch 2, sc in same sp, *[cl in next st, (sc in next st, cl in next st) across] to next corner ch-2 sp, (sc, ch 2, sc) in next corner ch sp; repeat from * 2 more times; repeat between [ ], join, **turn,** fasten off.

Rnd 5: Join rust with sc in any corner ch sp, sc in each st around with (sc, ch 2, sc) in each corner ch sp, join, **turn.**

Rnd 6: Sl st in next st, ch 4, skip next st, *(dc in next st, ch 1, skip next st) across to next corner ch sp, (dc, ch 2, dc) in next corner ch sp, ch 1, skip next st; repeat from * around, join with sl st in 3rd ch of ch-4, **turn.**

Rnd 7: Ch 1, sc in each st and in each ch-1 sp around with (sc, ch 2, sc) in each corner ch-2 sp, join with sl st in first sc, fasten off (29 sc across each short end between corner ch sps, 175 sc across each long edge between corner ch sps).

Holding Panels right sides together, matching sts, alternating Panels A and B, with rust, sew together through **back bars** (see illustration).

BORDER

Rnd 1: Working around entire outer edge, join dk. green with sc in any corner ch sp, ch 2, sc in same sp, sc in each st and in each seam around with (sc, ch 2, sc) in each corner ch sp, join with sl st in first sc, **turn,** fasten off (121 sc across each short end between corner ch-2 sps, 177 sc across each long edge between corner ch-2 sps).

Rnds 2-3: Repeat same rnds of Panel A Edging, ending with 125 sc across each short end between corner ch-2 sps and 181 sc across each long edge between corner ch-2 sps.

Rnd 4: Join rust with sc in any corner ch sp, ch 2, sc in same sp, *[tr in next st, (sc in next st, cl in next st, sc in next st, tr in next st) across] to next corner ch sp, (sc, ch 2, sc) in next corner ch sp; repeat from * 2 more times; repeat between [ ], join, **turn,** fasten off.

Rnd 5: Join dk. green with sc in any corner ch sp, ch 2, sc in same sp, sc in each st around with (sc, ch 2, sc) in each corner ch sp, join, **turn**.

Rnds 6-7: Repeat rnds 2 and 3 of Panel A Edging.◆

Firesides, Snow & Mistletoe

Chapter Seven

7.

Granny's Rose Trellis
Baby's Baubles
Christmas in the Country
San Antonio Blues
Christmas Pines
Christmas Senses
Old-Fashioned Christmas
Checking the Trees

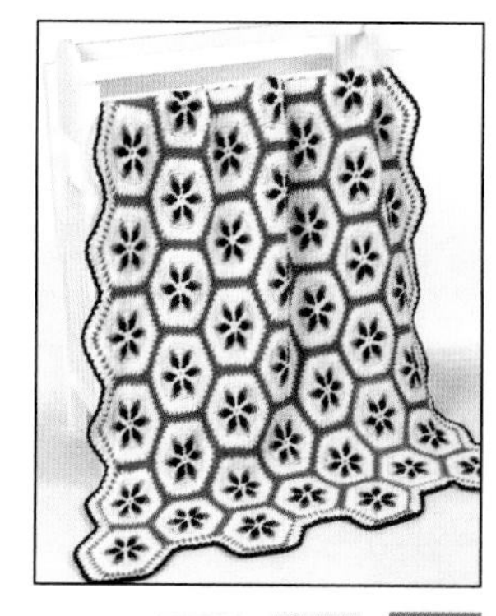

Recollections of snowflake decorated holly leaves and berries encourage fond moments in time, as all hearts and thoughts drift homeward for the holidays.

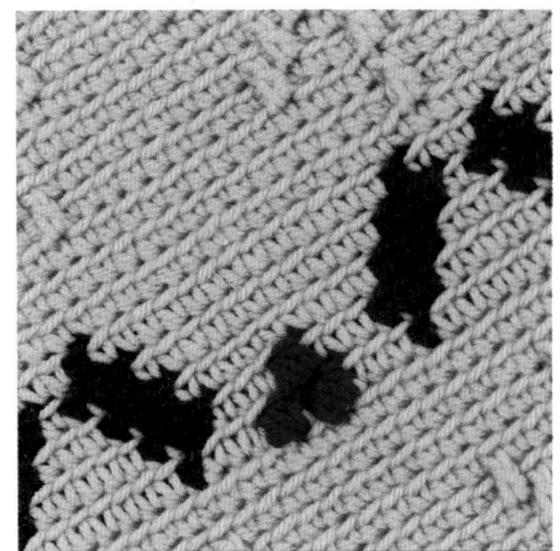

Christmas in the Country

by DIANA SIPPEL
of DIANA LYNN'S DESIGNS

SIZE: 42" x 51½".

MATERIALS: Worsted-weight yarn — 48 oz. buff, 5 oz. each burgundy and dk. spruce; H crochet hook or size needed to obtain gauge.

GAUGE: 11 sc = 3"; 3 sc rows worked in **back lps** = 1".

SKILL LEVEL: ☆☆ Average

AFGHAN

NOTES: *Work first 2 sts and last 2 sts of each row in* ***both lps.*** *Work each remaining st in* ***back lps*** *only.*

Do not *turn at the end of each row.*

Leave 2" end at the beginning and end of each row for Fringe.

For ***cluster (cl);*** *working in front of last row, yo, insert hook in* ***front lp*** *of next st on row before last, yo, draw lp through, yo, draw through 2 lps on hook, (yo, insert hook in* ***front lp*** *of same st on row before last, yo, draw lp through, yo, draw through 2 lps on hook) 2 times, drop burgundy, yo with buff, draw through all 4 lps on hook. Skip next st on last row behind cl.*

For ***long-double crochet (l-dc);*** *working in front of last row, yo, insert hook in* ***front lp*** *of next st on row before last, yo, draw lp through, (yo, draw through 2 lps on hook) 2 times. Skip next st on last row behind l-dc.*

For ***puff stitch (puff st),*** *yo, insert hook in* ***front lp*** *of next st, yo, draw up long lp, (yo, insert hook in* ***front lp*** *of same st, yo, draw up long lp) 2 times, yo, draw through all 7 lps on hook.*

When changing colors (see page 159), drop color to wrong side of work. Work over dropped color and pick up again when needed. Fasten off dropped color at end of each color section.

Each square on graph equals one st.

Work even rows on graph from right to left, then repeat same rows from left to right. Work center of row marked on graph only one time.

Row 1: With buff, ch 177, fasten off; join buff with sc in first ch, sc in each ch across, fasten off (177 sc).

Rows 2-3: Join buff with sc in first st, sc in each st across, fasten off.

Row 4: For **row 4 of graph** (see page 138), join buff with sc in first st, sc in next 12 sts changing to burgundy in last st made, *[cl, sc in next 5 sts changing to burgundy in last st made, cl, sc in next 9 sts changing to burgundy in last st made, sc in next st changing to buff, sc in next 9 sts changing to burgundy in last st made, cl, sc in next 5 sts

continued on next page

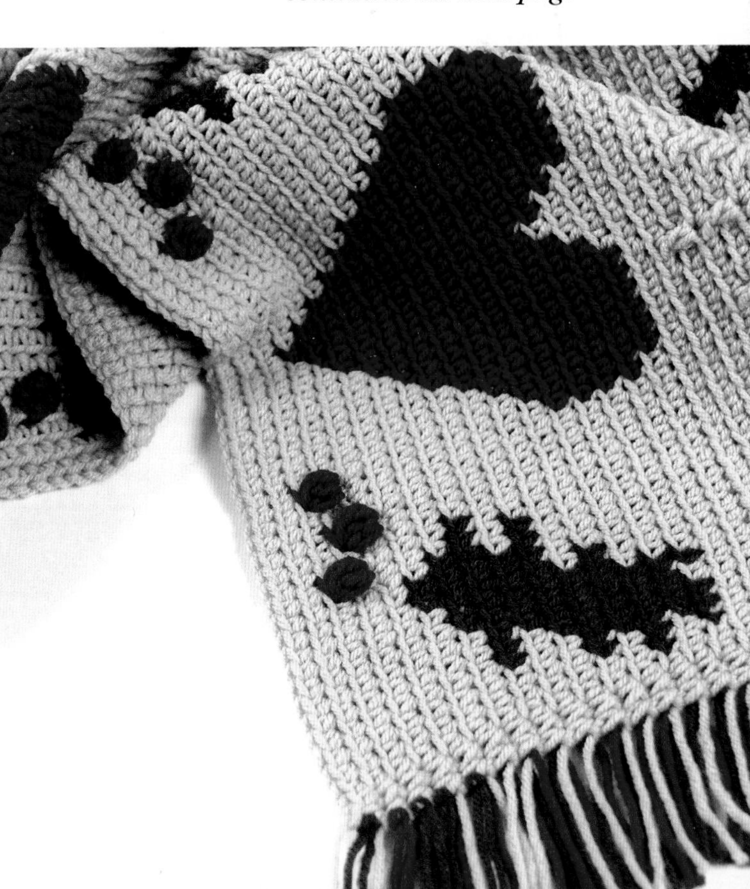

Christmas in the Country

Continued from page 137

changing to burgundy in last st made, cl], sc in next 26 sts changing to burgundy in last st made; repeat from *; repeat between [ ], sc in last 13 sts, fasten off.

Rows 5-53: Work according to graph.

Rows 54-133: Repeat rows 34-53 consecutively.

Rows 134-150: Work according to graph. At end of last row, fasten off.

FRINGE

For **each Fringe,** cut one strand of yarn 4½" long. Fold in half, insert hook in end of row, draw fold through, draw all loose ends through fold, tighten. Trim to 2".

Alternating dk. spruce and burgundy, work one Fringe in end of each row on each long edge of Afghan.◆

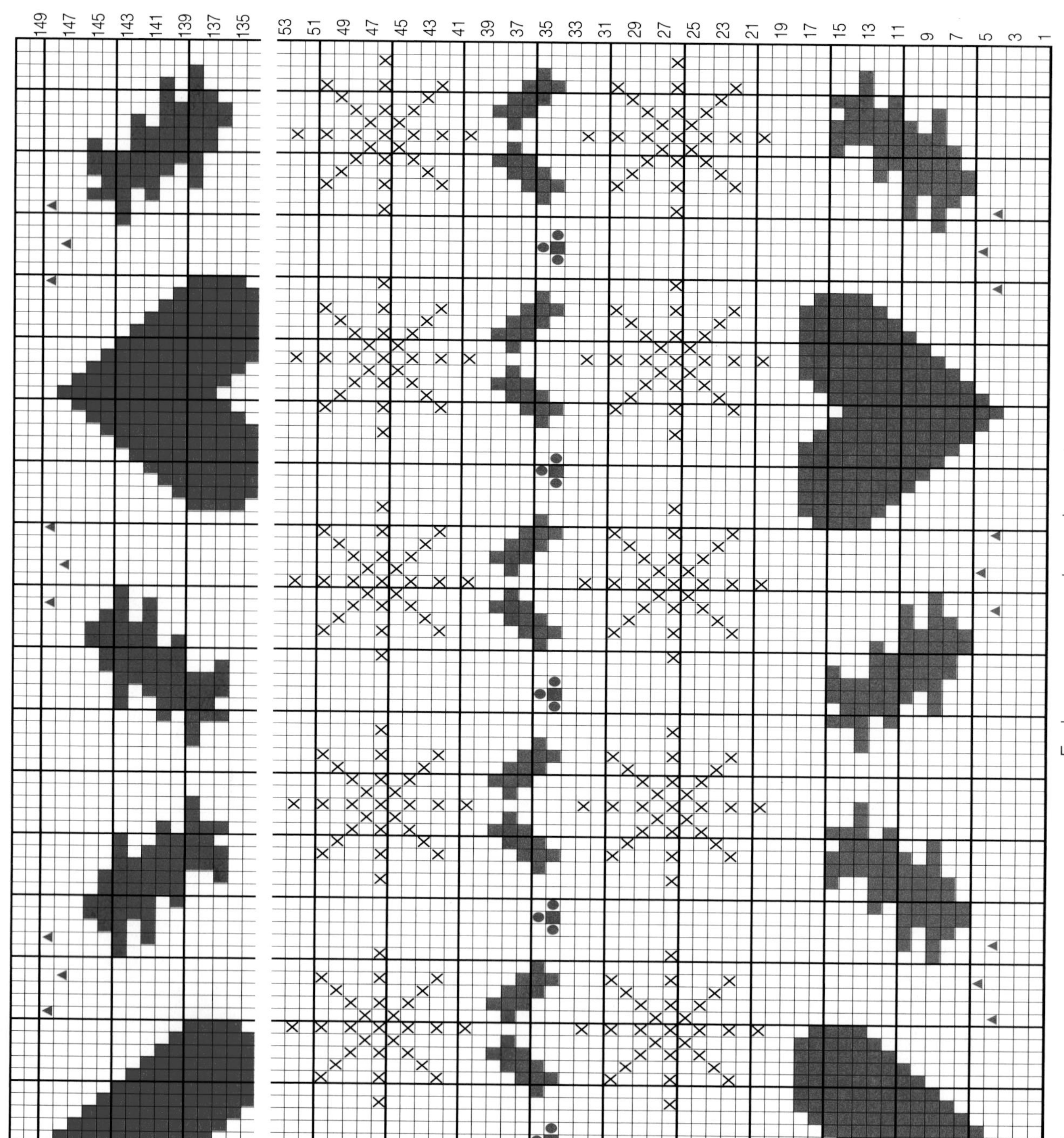

Decorate the tree with buttons this year, topped with a star and full of tradition, just dreaming of Santa and wishfully thinking.

Christmas Pines

by MAGGIE WELDON

SIZE: 45" x 63½".

MATERIALS: Worsted-weight yarn — 31½ oz. off-white, 21 oz. green, 7 oz. gold and 2 oz. rust; 160 flat buttons in assorted colors and sizes; craft glue or hot glue gun; tapestry needle; H crochet hook or size needed to obtain gauge.

GAUGE: 13 sc = 4"; 4 sc rows = 1". Each Block is 11" x 12½".

SKILL LEVEL: ☆☆ Average

BLOCK (make 20)

Row 1: With off-white, ch 28, sc in 2nd ch from hook, sc in each ch across, turn (27 sc).

Row 2: Ch 1, sc in each st across, turn.

NOTES:** When changing colors (see page 159), always drop yarn to wrong side of work. Use a separate skein or ball of yarn for each color section.* ***Do not *carry yarn across from one section to another. Fasten off colors at end of each color section.*

Work odd-numbered graph rows from right to left and even-numbered rows from left to right.

Each square on graph equals one sc.

Row 3: For **row 3 of graph** (see page 147), ch 1, sc in first 12 sts changing to rust in last st made, sc in each of next 3 sts changing to off-white in last st made, sc in last 12 sts, turn.

Rows 4-38: Ch 1, sc in each st across changing colors according to graph, turn. At end of last row, **do not** turn.

Rnd 39: Working around outer edge, ch 1, evenly space 27 sc across ends of rows; working in starting ch on opposite side of row 1, 3 sc in first ch, sc in each ch across with 3 sc in last ch, evenly space 27 sc across ends of rows, 3 sc in first st, sc in each st across with 3 sc in last st, join with sl st in first sc, **turn,** fasten off (27 sc across each short end between corner sc, 29 sc across each long edge between corner sc).

Rnd 40: Join gold with sc in any st, sc in each st around with 3 sc in each center corner st, join, **do not** turn, fasten off (27 sc across each short end between corner sts, 29 sc across each long edge between corner sts).

Rnd 41: With off-white, repeat rnd 40.

Rnd 42: Join green with sl st in any center corner st, ch 3, (dc, ch 2, 2 dc) in same st, skip next st, (2 dc in next st, skip next st) across to next center corner st, *(2 dc, ch 2, 2 dc) in next center corner st, skip next st, (2 dc in next st, skip next st) across to next center corner st; repeat from * around, join with sl st in top of ch-3, fasten off.

Holding Blocks wrong sides together, matching

continued on page 147

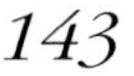

Keep Santa warm while he spreads good cheer, going roof to roof with his little reindeer. Ho! Ho! Merry Christmas! and Happy New Year!

Christmas Senses

by KATHERINE ENG

SIZE: 43" x 61".

MATERIALS: Worsted-weight yarn — 20 oz. each white and green fleck, 8 oz. each med. green and red fleck; H crochet hook or size needed to obtain gauge.

GAUGE: Rnds 1-2 of Square = 2¼" across. Each Square is 6" across.

SKILL LEVEL: ☆☆ Average

FIRST ROW

First Square

Rnd 1: With white, ch 4, sl st in first ch to form ring, ch 1, 8 sc in ring, join with sl st in first sc (8 sc).

Rnd 2: Ch 1, (sc, ch 3, sc) in first st, ch 1, *(sc, ch 3, sc) in next st, ch 1; repeat from * around, join, **turn,** fasten off (8 ch-3 sps, 8 ch-1 sps).

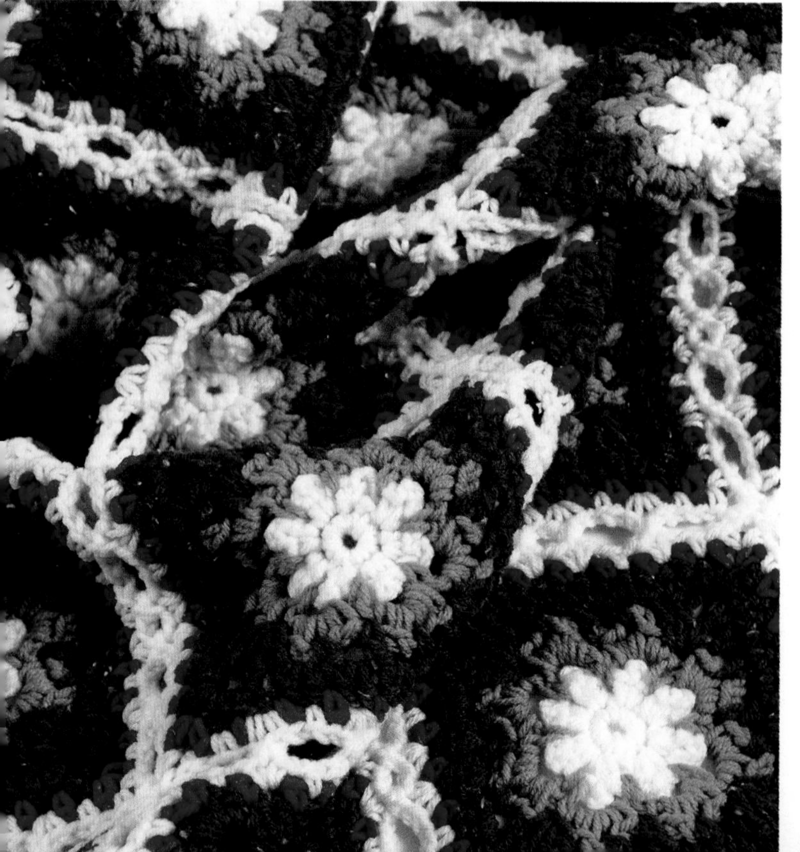

Rnd 3: Join med. green with sc in any ch-1 sp, ch 3, (sc in next ch-1 sp, ch 3) around, join, **turn** (8 ch-3 sps).

Rnd 4: Sl st in next ch sp, ch 1, (2 sc, ch 2, 2 sc) in same sp, ch 1, *(2 sc, ch 2, 2 sc) in next ch sp, ch 1; repeat from * around, join, **do not** turn, fasten off (8 ch-2 sps, 8 ch-1 sps).

Rnd 5: Join green fleck with sl st in any ch-1 sp, ch 3, (dc, ch 3, 2 dc) in same sp, *[ch 1, sc in next ch-2 sp, ch 1, dc in next ch-1 sp, ch 1, sc in next ch-2 sp, ch 1], (2 dc, ch 3, 2 dc) in next ch-1 sp; repeat from * 2 more times; repeat between [ ], join with sl st in top of ch-3, **turn** (28 sts, 16 ch-1 sps, 4 ch-3 sps).

Rnd 6: Ch 1, sc in each st and in each ch-1 sp around with (2 sc, ch 2, 2 sc) in each corner ch-3 sp, join with sl st in first sc, **turn,** fasten off (15 sc on each side between corner ch sps).

Rnd 7: Join red fleck with sc in any corner ch sp, ch 2, sc in same sp, *[ch 1, skip next st, (sc in next st, ch 1, skip next st) across] to next corner ch sp, (sc, ch 2, sc) in next corner ch sp; repeat from * 2 more times; repeat between [ ], join, **do not** turn, fasten off.

Rnd 8: Join white with sc in any corner ch sp, ch 4, sc in same sp, [◊*ch 1, sc in next ch sp, ch 1, (sc, ch 2, sc) in next ch sp, ch 1, sc in next ch sp, ch 1*, (sc, ch 2, sc) in each of next 2 ch sps; repeat between **◊, (sc, ch 4, sc) in next corner ch sp]; repeat between [ ] 2 more times; repeat between ◊◊, join, fasten off.

Second Square

Rnds 1-7: Repeat same rnds of First Square.

NOTES: *For **joining ch-4 sp,** ch 2, drop lp from hook, insert hook in corresponding ch-4 sp on other Square, draw dropped lp through, ch 2.*

continued on page 146

Christmas Senses

Continued from page 144

*For **joining ch-2 sp**, ch 1, drop lp from hook, insert hook in corresponding ch-2 sp on other Square, draw dropped lp through, ch 1.*

Rnd 8: Join white with sc in any corner ch sp; joining to side of last Square on this row, work joining ch-4 sp, sc in same sp on this Square, ch 1, sc in next ch sp, ch 1, sc in next ch sp, work joining ch-2 sp, sc in same sp on this Square, ch 1, sc in next ch sp, ch 1, (sc in next ch sp, work joining ch-2 sp, sc in same sp on this Square) 2 times, ch 1, sc in next ch sp, ch 1, sc in next ch sp, work joining ch-2 sp, sc in same sp on this Square, ch 1, sc in next ch sp, ch 1, sc in next corner ch sp, work joining ch-4 sp, sc in same sp on this Square, [◊*ch 1, sc in next ch sp, ch 1, (sc, ch 2, sc) in next ch sp, ch 1, sc in next ch sp, ch 1*, (sc, ch 2, sc) in each of next 2 ch sps; repeat between **◊, (sc, ch 4, sc) in next corner ch sp]; repeat between [ ]; repeat between ◊◊, join, fasten off.

Repeat Second Square 5 more times for a total of 7 Squares on this row.

SECOND ROW

First Square

Joining to bottom of First Square on last row, work same as First Row Second Square on page 144.

Second Square

Rnds 1-7: Repeat same rnds of First Row First Square on page 144.

Rnd 8: Join white with sc in any corner ch sp; joining to bottom of next Square on last row, work joining ch-4 sp, sc in same sp on this Square, *ch 1, sc in next ch sp, ch 1, sc in next ch sp, work joining ch-2 sp, sc in same sp on this Square, ch 1, sc in next ch sp, ch 1, (sc in next ch sp, work joining ch-2 sp, sc in same sp on this Square) 2 times, ch 1, sc in next ch sp, ch 1, sc in next ch sp, work joining ch-2 sp, sc in same sp on this Square, ch 1, sc in next ch sp, ch 1, sc in next corner ch sp, work joining ch-4 sp, sc in same sp on this Square*; joining to side of last Motif on this row, repeat between **, [◊ch 1, sc in next ch sp, ch 1, (sc, ch 2, sc) in next ch sp, ch 1, sc in next ch sp, ch 1], (sc, ch 2, sc) in each of next 2 ch sps; repeat between [ ]◊, (sc, ch 4, sc) in next corner ch sp; repeat between ◊◊, join, fasten off.

Repeat Second Square 5 more times for a total of 7 Squares on this row.

Repeat Second Row 8 more times for a total of 10 rows.

EDGING

Working around entire outer edge, join white with sc in any corner ch sp, (hdc, 3 dc, hdc, sc) in same sp, ◊•*[ch 2, skip next ch sp, sc in next ch sp, (hdc, 3 dc, hdc) in next ch sp, sc in next ch sp, ch 1, skip next ch sp, (sc, ch 2, sc) in each of next 2 ch sps, ch 1, skip next ch sp, sc in next ch sp, (hdc, 3 dc, hdc) in next ch sp, sc in next ch sp, ch 2, skip next ch sp], (sc, ch 2, sc) in each of next 2 joined ch-4 sps; repeat from * across to next last Motif on this edge; repeat between [ ]•, (sc, hdc, 3 dc, hdc, sc) in next corner ch sp; repeat from ◊ 2 more times; repeat between ••, join with sl st in first sc, fasten off.◆

San Antonio Blues

Continued from page 140

join with sl st in first sc, **turn.**

Rnd 2: Sl st in next st, ch 1, sc in same st, *ch 1, skip next st, (sc in next st, ch 1, skip next st) across to next corner ch sp, (sc, ch 3, sc) in next corner ch sp; repeat from * around to last st, ch 1, skip last st, join, **turn,** fasten off.

Rnd 3: Join teal with sl st in any corner ch-3 sp, ch 4, (dc, ch 2, dc, ch 1, dc) in same sp, ch 1, (dc in next ch-1 sp, ch 1) across to next corner ch-3 sp, *(dc, ch 1, dc, ch 2, dc, ch 1, dc) in next corner ch-3 sp, ch 1, (dc in next ch-1 sp, ch 1) across to next corner ch-3 sp; repeat from * around, join with sl st in 3rd ch of ch-4, **turn.**

Rnd 4: Sl st in next ch-1 sp, ch 1, sc in same sp, *ch 1, (sc in next ch-1 sp, ch 1) across to next corner ch-2 sp, (sc, ch 2, sc) in next corner ch-2 sp; repeat from * around to last ch-1 sp, ch 1, sc in last ch sp, ch 1, join with sl st in first sc, **turn.**

Rnd 5: Sl st in first ch-1 sp, ch 1, (sc, ch 2, sc) in same sp, (sc, ch 2, sc) in each ch-1 sp around with (sc, ch 2, sc, ch 3, sc, ch 2, sc) in each corner ch-2 sp around, join, fasten off.◆

Christmas Pines

Continued from page 143

sts, with green, sew together through **back lps** in 4 rows of 5 Blocks each.

Glue 8 buttons over each tree as desired.

EDGING

Working around entire outer edge, join green with sl st in any corner ch sp, ch 3, (dc, ch 2, 2 dc) in same sp, 2 dc in sp between each 2-dc group and in each seam around with (2 dc, ch 2, 2 dc) in each corner ch sp, join with sl st in top of ch-3, fasten off.◆

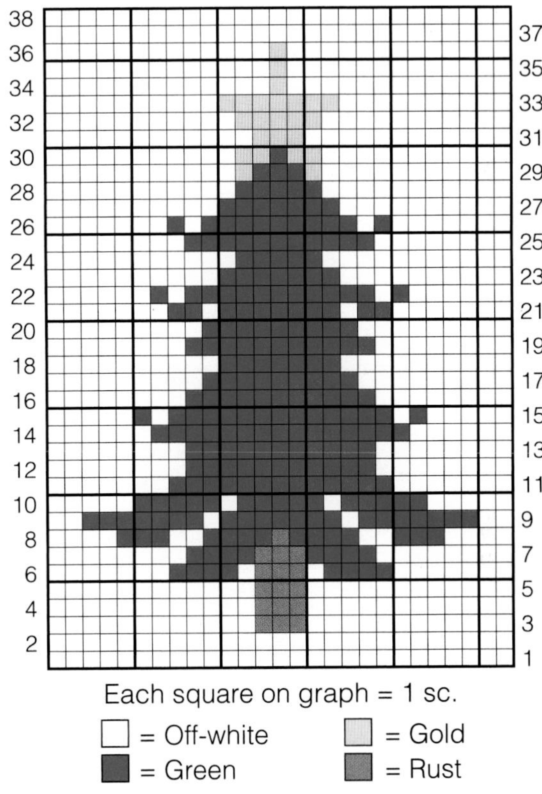

During the hustle and bustle, slip away for some quiet time, as merry motifs with burgundy petals tipped in green create a relaxed mood of cozy comfort.

Old-Fashioned Christmas

by DIANA SIPPEL
of DIANA LYNN'S DESIGNS

SIZE: 43" x 51".

MATERIALS: Worsted-weight yarn — 33 oz. natural, 6 oz. green and 3½ oz. burgundy; tapestry needle; H crochet hook or size needed to obtain gauge.

GAUGE: Rnds 1-5 of Motif = 3¾" across. Each Motif is 6¼" across.

SKILL LEVEL: ☆☆☆ Advanced

MOTIF (make 53)

Rnd 1: With natural, ch 5, sl st in first ch to form ring, ch 1, 12 sc in ring, join with sl st in first sc (12 sc).

*NOTE: Work rnds 2-5 in **back lps** only.*

Rnd 2: Ch 1, 2 sc in each st around, join (24).

Rnd 3: Ch 1, sc in each st around, join.

NOTES: When changing colors (see page 159), work over dropped color and pick up again when needed.

*For **first petal;** working in front of last rnd, yo, insert hook in **front lp** of 3rd st on rnd 2, yo, draw lp through, yo, draw through 2 lps on hook, yo, insert hook in **front lp** of next st on rnd 1, yo, draw up long lp, yo, draw through 2 lps on hook, yo, insert hook in **front lp** of 5th st on rnd 2, yo, draw lp through, yo, draw through 2 lps on hook, drop burgundy, with natural, draw through all 4 lps on hook. Skip next st on last rnd behind petal.*

*For **petal;** working in front of last rnd, skip next st on rnd 2, yo, insert hook in **front lp** of next st, yo, draw lp through, yo, draw through 2 lps on hook, skip next st on rnd 1, yo, insert hook in **front lp** of next st on rnd 1, yo, draw up long lp, yo, draw through 2 lps on hook, skip next st on rnd 2 behind center part of petal, yo, insert hook in **front lp** of next st, yo, draw lp through, yo, draw through 2 lps on hook, drop burgundy, with natural, draw through all 4 lps on hook. Skip next st on last rnd behind petal.*

Rnd 4: Ch 1, 2 sc in each of first 3 sts changing to burgundy in last st made, work first petal, (2 sc in each of next 3 sts changing to burgundy in last st made, work petal) around, join (36 sc, 6 petals).

*NOTE: For **leaf,** yo, insert hook in **front lp** of st before next petal on rnd 3, yo, draw lp through, yo, draw through 2 lps on hook, yo, insert hook in **front lp** of st after same petal on rnd 3, yo, draw lp through, yo, draw through 2 lps on hook, drop green, with natural, yo, draw through all 3 lps on hook. Skip next st on last rnd behind leaf.*

Rnd 5: Ch 1, sc in first 6 sts changing to green in last st made, work leaf, (sc in next 6 sts changing to

continued on page 153

Fun and frolicking in the snow, playful trees blowing to and fro, snowflakes drifting all the while, while checkered squares deck the halls in style.

Checking the Trees

by MARTHA BROOKS STEIN

SIZE: 42½" x 57½".

MATERIALS: Worsted yarn — 28 oz. white, 10 oz. green, 8 oz. red; tapestry needle; H and I crochet hooks or size needed to obtain gauge.

GAUGE: With **I hook,** each square = 2½" across.

SKILL LEVEL: ☆☆ Average

SOLID SQUARE
(make 139 white, 70 green, 36 red)

Rnd 1: With I hook, ch 4, sl st in first ch to form ring, ch 3, 2 dc in ring, (ch 2, 3 dc in ring) 3 times; to **join,** ch 1, dc in top of ch-3 (12 dc, 4 ch sps).

Rnd 2: Ch 3, 2 dc around joining dc, *ch 1, (3 dc, ch 2, 3 dc) in next ch sp; repeat from * 2 more times, ch 1, 3 dc in same sp as first ch-3, ch 2, join with sl st in top of ch-3, fasten off *(*24 dc, 8 ch sps).

HALF COLORED SQUARE (make 56)

Rnd 1: With I hook and white, ch 4, sl st in first ch to form ring, ch 3, (2 dc, ch 2, 3 dc) in ring, ch 1 changing to green (see illustration), ch 1, (3 dc, ch 2, 3 dc) in ring, ch 1 changing to white; to **join,** dc in top of ch-3 (12 dc, 4 ch sps).

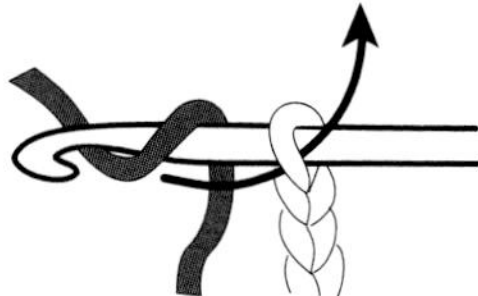

Rnd 2: Ch 3, 2 dc around joining dc, ch 1, (3 dc, ch 2, 3 dc) in next ch sp, ch 1, 3 dc in next ch sp, ch 1 changing to green, ch 1, 3 dc in same ch sp, ch 1, (3 dc, ch 2, 3 dc) in next ch sp, ch 1, 3 dc in same ch sp as first ch-3, ch 1 changing to white, ch 1, join with sl st in top of ch-3, fasten off.

QUARTER COLORED SQUARE (make 14)

Rnd 1: With I hook and white, ch 4, sl st in first ch to form ring, ch 3, 2 dc in ring, (ch 2, 3 dc in ring) 2 times, ch 1 changing to green, ch 1, 3 dc in ring, ch 1 changing to white; to **join,** dc in top of ch-3 (12 dc, 4 ch sps).

Rnd 2: Ch 3, 2 dc around joining dc, *ch 1, (3 dc, ch 2, 3 dc) in next ch sp; repeat from *, ch 1, 3 dc in next ch sp, ch 1 changing to green, ch 1, 3 dc in same ch sp, ch 1, 3 dc in same ch sp as first ch-3, ch 1 changing to white, ch 1, join with sl st in top of ch-3, fasten off.

Holding Squares wrong sides together, match-

continued on page 152

Checking the Trees

Continued from page 150

ing sts, with matching color, sew together through **back lps** according to Assembly Illustration.

BORDER

Rnd 1: Working around entire outer edge in **back lps** only, with H hook and red, join with sc in 2nd ch of corner ch sp before one short end, *[sc in each st, in each ch and in each ch on each side of seams across to next corner ch-2 sp, sc in next ch, ch 2], sc in next ch; repeat from * 2 more times; repeat between [ ], join with sl st in first sc (135 sc across each short end between corner ch sps, 189 sc across each long edge between corner ch sps).

Rnd 2: Ch 4, skip next st, *(dc in next 3 sts, ch 1, skip next st) across to st before next corner ch sp, dc in next st, (2 dc ch 3, 2 dc) in next ch sp, skip next st, dc in next st, ch 1, skip next st, (dc in next 3 sts, ch 1, skip next st) across to 2 sts before next corner ch sp, dc in next 2 sts, (dc, ch 3, 2 dc) in next corner ch sp)*, dc in next st, ch 2, skip next st; repeat between **, join with sl st in 4th ch of ch-5.

Rnd 3: Sl st in next ch sp, ch 3, 2 dc in same sp, ch 1, (3 dc, ch 1) in each ch sp around with (3 dc, ch 2, 3 dc, ch 1) in each corner ch sp, join with sl st in top of ch-3.

Rnds 4-5: Sl st in next 2 sts, sl st in next ch sp, ch 3, 2 dc in same sp, ch 1, (3 dc, ch 1) in each ch sp around with (3 dc, ch 2, 3 dc, ch 1) in each corner ch sp, join with sl st in top of ch-3. At end of last rnd, fasten off.

Rnd 6: Join white with sc in any ch sp, ch 2; working from left to right, **reverse sc** (see page 158) in center st of next 3-dc group, ch 2, (reverse sc in next ch sp, ch 2, reverse sc in center st of next 3-dc group, ch 2) around, join with sl st in first sc, fasten off.◆

ASSEMBLY ILLUSTRATON

Old-Fashioned Christmas

Continued from page 149

green in last st made, work leaf) around, join.

Rnd 6: Working the following rnds in **both lps,** ch 1, sc in each st around, join (42 sc).

Rnd 7: Ch 3, dc in next 5 sts, (3 dc, ch 1, 3 dc) in next st, *dc in next 6 sts, (3 dc, ch 1, 3 dc) in next st; repeat from * around, join with sl st in top of ch-3, fasten off (72 dc, 6 ch sps).

Rnd 8: Join green with sc in any ch sp, ch 1, sc in same sp, (ch 1, skip next st, sc in next st) 6 times, ch 1, *(sc, ch 1, sc) in next ch sp, (ch 1, skip next st, sc in next st) 6 times, ch 1; repeat from * around, join with sl st in first sc, fasten off (48 sc, 48 ch sps).

Holding Motifs wrong sides together, matching sts, with green, sew together through **back lps** according to Assembly Diagram.

BORDER

Rnd 1: Working around entire outer edge, join natural with sl st in first ch sp after seam on first Motif before one short end (see diagram), ch 3, dc in same sp, 2 dc in each of next 6 ch sps, [3 dc in next ch sp, 2 dc in each of next 7 ch sps, ch 3, (sl st in next ch sp, ch 3) 9 times, *(2 dc in each of next 7 ch sps, dc ch sps before and after next seam tog) 2 times, 2 dc in each of next 7 ch sps, ch 3, (sl st in next ch sp, ch 3) 9 times; repeat from * 2 more times, (2 dc in each of next 7 ch sps, 3 dc in next ch sp, 2 dc in each of next 7 ch sps, dc ch sps before and after next seam tog) 7 times], 2 dc in each of next 7 ch sps; repeat between [ ], join with sl st in top of ch-3.

Rnd 2: Sl st in next st, ch 3, [skip next st, (sl st in next st, ch 3, skip next st) across to next ch sp, (sl st in next ch sp, ch 3) 10 times, *(sl st in next st, ch 3, skip next st) across to next ch sp, (sl st in next ch sp, ch 3) 10 times; repeat from * 2 more times]; repeat between [ ], skip next st, (sl st in next st, ch 3, skip next st) across, join with sl st in first sl st, fasten off.

Rnd 3: Join burgundy with sl st in any ch sp, ch 2, (sl st in next ch sp, ch 2) around, join, fasten off.◆

ASSEMBLY DIAGRAM

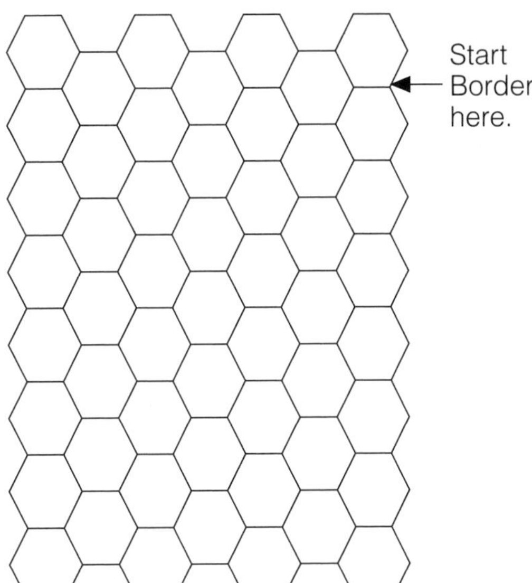

This book has been written in such a way that anyone, regardless of their experience, can enjoy making these patterns. Before you begin, please read the helpful information included in the next few pages to familiarize yourself with methods, terms and techniques referred to in the instructions. All basic stitches are included in the illustrated Stitch Guide. Special terms and stitches are listed in the applicable patterns.

Getting Started

Yarn & Hooks

When shopping for yarn, be sure to check the label for the weight specification. By using the weight of yarn specified in the pattern, you will be assured of achieving the proper gauge. It is best to purchase at least one extra skein of each color needed to allow for differences in tension and dyes.

For a neat, professional finish to your afghan, using the same brand of yarn for each color needed will enhance the looks of your work. Fiber and dye variations from one manufacturer to another can cause yarn to look and feel very different, which affects the texture and gauge of your work. If you must mix brand names to attain the colors you need, be sure to compare the yarns closely for consistency and weight, choosing the ones that are the most similar.

The hook size stated in the pattern is to be used as a guide for determining the hook size you will need. Before beginning the actual pattern, always work a swatch of an afghan's stitch pattern with the suggested hook size to check your gauge. If you find your gauge is smaller or larger than what is specified in the pattern, choose a different size hook.

Gauge

Gauge is probably the most important aspect of creating a beautiful afghan that mirrors the one in the photograph. If your gauge is too large or too small, your finished piece will probably look very different from the original.

Gauge is measured by counting the number of rows or stitches per inch. Each of the afghans featured in this book will have a gauge listed. In some patterns, gauge for small motifs or flowers is given as an overall measurement. Gauge must be attained in order for the afghan to come out the size stated, and to prevent ruffling and puckering. Usually a finished size for blocks, motifs or strips will also be given. This will help you double-check your gauge in the end.

To check your gauge, make a swatch about 4" square in the stitch indicated in the gauge section of the instructions. Lay

the swatch flat and measure the stitches over the space of several inches. If you have more stitches per inch than specified in the pattern, your gauge is too tight and you need a larger hook. Fewer stitches per inch indicates a gauge that is too loose. In this case, choose the next smaller hook size.

Next, check the number of rows. Generally, if the stitch gauge is achieved, the row gauge will also be correct. However, due to differing crochet techniques and hook styles, you may find your stitch gauge is right, but your row gauge is not. Most crocheters with this problem achieve the stitch gauge, but find their row gauge is too short. In either case, don't change hooks, but rather adjust your row gauge by pulling the loops down a little tighter on your hook to shorten them, or by pulling the first loop up slightly to extend them.

Once you've attained the proper gauge, you're ready to start your afghan. Remember to check your gauge periodically to avoid problems when it's time to assemble the pieces, to prevent the edges of your afghan from having a wavy or V'd appearance. If you begin to notice your work getting larger or smaller, compensate by changing hooks. It is common for crocheters to "loosen up" on the gauge as they gradually become familiar with a pattern. Changing to the next size smaller hook will remedy this nicely.

Reading & Repeating

Before beginning a new pattern, read through it to familiarize yourself with the various stitches used, any notes or unusual stitches that appear or are new to you. Special instructions are typically bolded to draw your attention to them, and the stitches shown at the end of a row or round in parentheses are the stitch count for that particular row or round. Stitch counts are given so that you can check your progress on each row or round to verify its accuracy.

Written crochet instructions typically include symbols such as parentheses, asterisks and brackets used to repeat sections of the instructions. In some patterns, a fourth symbol, usually a diamond, may be added, and in rare cases a fifth symbol, typically a large dot (known as a bullet), will be used. These symbols are signposts added to set off a portion of instructions that will be worked more than once.

Parentheses ( ) enclose instructions which are to be worked the number of times indicated after the parentheses. For example, "(2 dc in next st, skip next st) 5 times" means to follow the instructions within the parentheses a total of five times. Parentheses may also be used to enclose a group of stitches which should be worked in one space or stitch. For example, "(2 dc, ch 2, 2 dc) in next st" means to work all the stitches within the parentheses in the next stitch.

Asterisks * may be used alone or in pairs, most times in combination with parentheses. If used in pairs, a set of instructions enclosed within asterisks will be followed by instructions for repeating. These repeat instructions may appear later in the pattern or immediately after the last asterisk. For example, "*Dc in next 4 sts, (2 dc, ch 2, 2 dc) in corner sp*, dc in next 4 sts; repeat between ** 2 more times" means to work through the instructions up to the word "repeat," then repeat only the instructions that are enclosed within the asterisks twice.

If used alone, an asterisk marks the beginning of instructions which are to be repeated. For example, "Ch 2, dc in same st, ch 2, *dc in next st, (ch 2, skip next 2 sts, dc in next st) 5 times; repeat from * across" means to work from the beginning, then repeat only the instructions after the *, working all the way across the row. Instructions for repeating may also specify a number of times to repeat, followed by further instructions. In this instance, work through the instructions one time, then repeat the number of times stated, then follow the remainder of the instructions.

Brackets [ ] and diamonds ◊ are used in the same manner as asterisks. Follow the specific instructions given when repeating. Sometimes, all four repeat symbols will appear in the same row or round. Simply follow the instructions as they are written, letting the symbols lead you. There is no need to be intimidated by lots of symbols. When followed carefully, these signposts will get you where you're going — to the end of a beautiful finished project.

For patterns with numerous repeats that can get confusing, there are several methods for marking your place for quick recognition of where you are. A few of these methods are: Mark the end of each repeat with a bobby pin; at the end of 5 or 10 repeats, remove all but the last pin. Or, keep a pad and pencil handy and make a hash-mark after completing each repeat. To tame extremely complicated patterns, write each set of instructions out on a 3" x 5" card so you can't lose your place in a long row or round.

Finishing

Patterns that require assembly will suggest a tapestry needle in the materials. This should be a #16 or #18 blunt-tipped tapestry needle. Sharp-pointed needles are not appropriate, as they can cut the yarn and weaken the stitches. When stitching pieces together, be careful to keep the seams flat so pieces do not pucker at the seams.

Hiding loose ends is never a fun task, but if done correctly may mean the difference between an afghan that looks great for years, or one that soon shows signs of wear. Always leave about 6-8" when beginning or ending. Thread the loose end into your tapestry needle and carefully weave the end through the back of several stitches. Then, to assure a secure hold, weave in the opposite direction, going through different strands. Gently pull the end, and clip, allowing the end to pull up under the stitches.

If your afghan needs blocking, a light steam pressing works well. Lay your afghan on a large table or on the floor, shaping and smoothing by hand as much as possible. Adjust your steam iron to the permanent press setting, then hold slightly above the stitches, allowing the steam to penetrate the yarn. Do not rest the iron on the afghan. Allow to dry completely.

Most afghans do not require professional blocking, but if this is your preference, choose a cleaning service that specializes in needlework. Request blocking only if you

do not want the afghan dry cleaned, and attach fringe or tassels after blocking.

Many of the designs featured in this book require fringe, so here are a few tips for the best-looking fringe possible.

To make cutting large numbers of strands for fringe easier, use a piece of cardboard half the length of the strand needed and about 6-8" wide. Wrap the yarn around the cardboard, moving across the width, being careful not to stretch the yarn. To assure an even length, try not to layer too many wraps on top of each other. After you have finished wrapping, cut the strands at one edge of the cardboard, and you're ready to begin fringing.

Make sure the yarn for the fringe is straight before cutting. If you are using the inside of a skein and the yarn is crinkled, wrap it around the cardboard, then steam lightly to remove wrinkles and allow to dry. Re-wrap if necessary.

Trimming ends can also be a breeze if you utilize a quilter's straight edge and rotary fabric cutter. These tools are commonly available at most large fabric or variety stores and are well worth the cost if you frequently make afghans with fringe.

To use a rotary cutter, fringe the entire edge of the afghan, but do not trim the ends. Now, lay the afghan on a flat, sturdy surface over a cutting mat suitable for use with rotary cutters. Using a large-toothed comb, gently straighten the fringe strands, then lay the straight edge over the fringe where you want to cut. Simply press the cutter into the yarn and roll along the straight edge. You will have neatly cut, perfectly even fringe that looks great.

For More Information

Sometimes even the most experienced needlecrafters can find themselves having trouble following instructions. If you have difficulty completing your project, write to:

Afghan Splendor Editors
The Needlecraft Shop
23 Old Pecan Road, Big Sandy, Texas 75755

Stitch Guide

Chain (ch)

Yo, draw hook through lp.

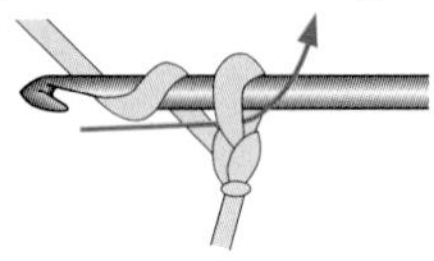

Slip Stitch (sl st)

Insert hook in st, yo, draw through st and lp on hook.

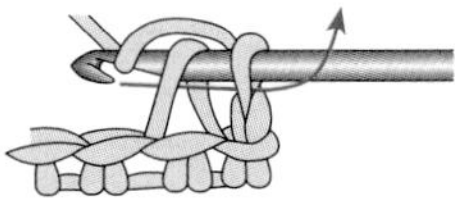

Treble Crochet (tr)

Yo 2 times, insert hook in st (a), yo, draw lp through (b), (yo, draw through 2 lps on hook) 3 times (c, d and e).

a

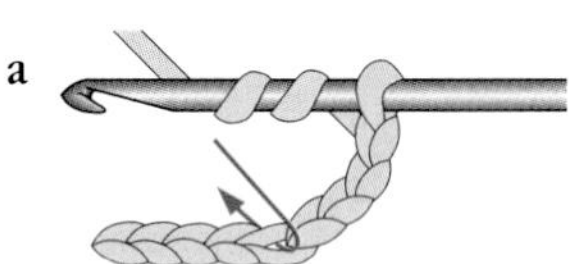

b

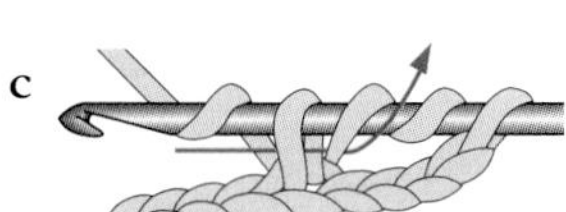

c

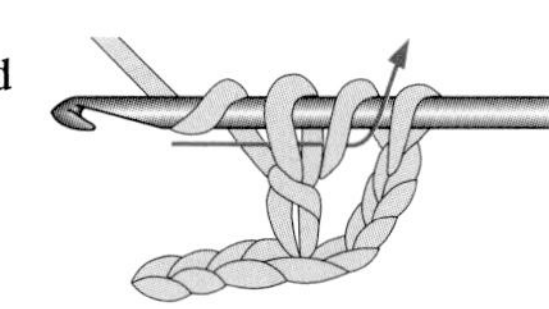

d

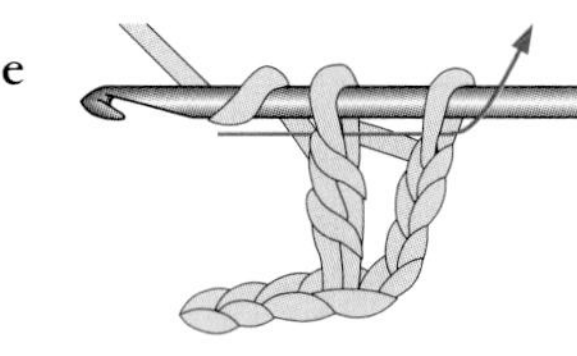

e

Single Crochet (sc)

Insert hook in st (a), yo, draw lp through, yo, draw through both lps on hook (b).

a

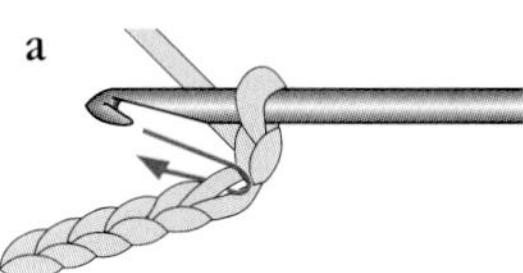

b

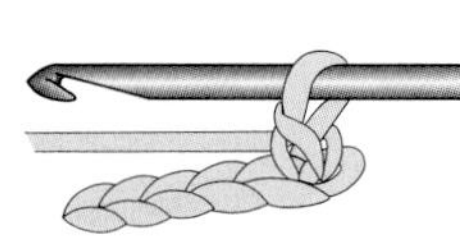

Double Crochet (dc)

Yo, insert hook in st (a), yo, draw lp through (b), (yo, draw through 2 lps on hook) 2 times (c and d).

a

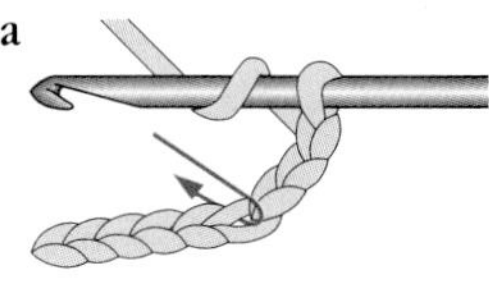

b

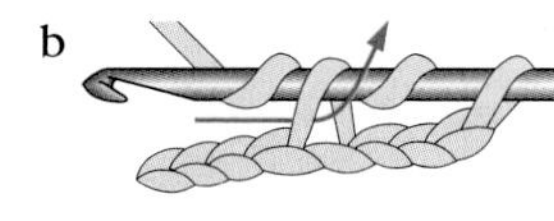

c

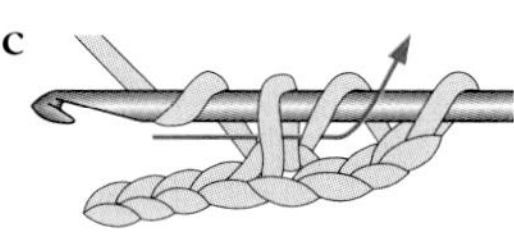

d

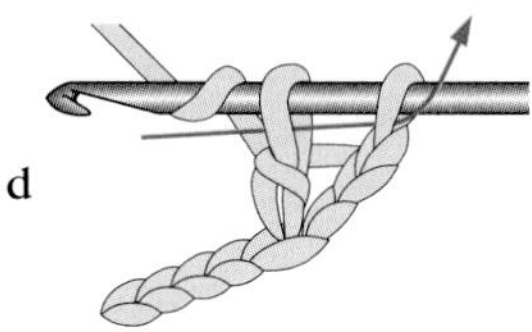

Double Treble Crochet (dtr)

Yo 3 times, insert hook in st (a), yo, draw lp through (b), (yo, draw through 2 lps on hook) 4 times (c, d, e and f).

a

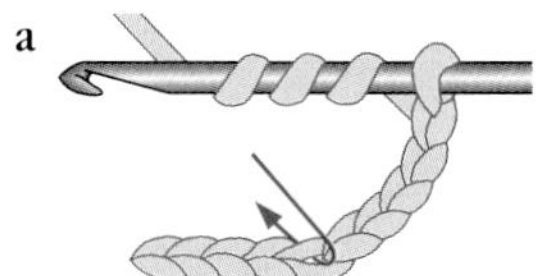

b

c

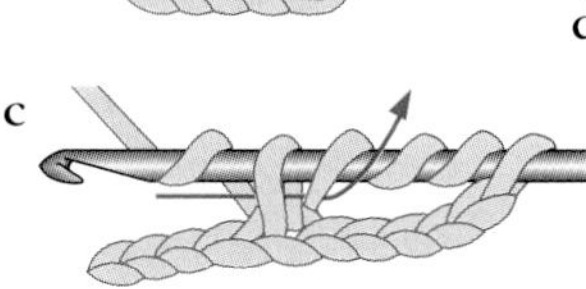

d

e

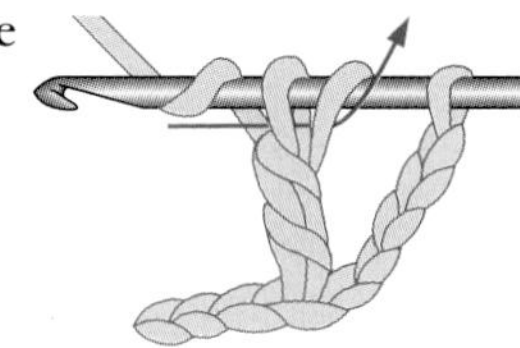

f

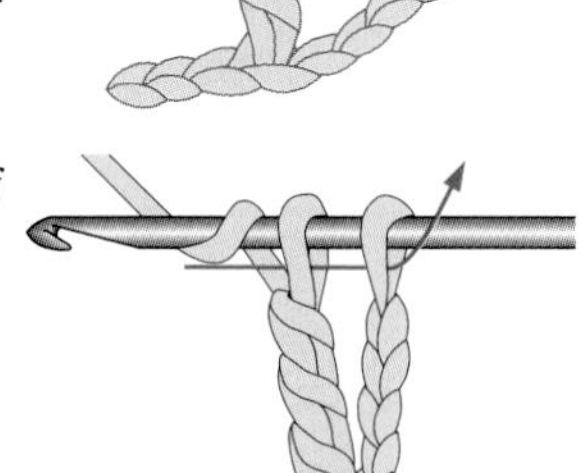

Half Double Crochet (hdc)

Yo, insert hook in st (a), yo, draw lp through (b), yo, draw through all 3 lps on hook (c).

a

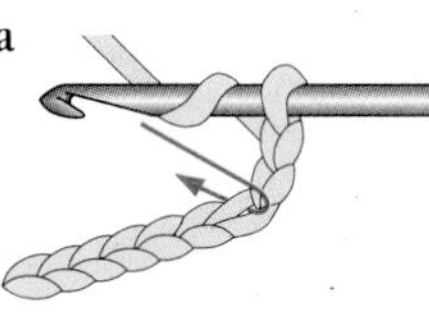

b

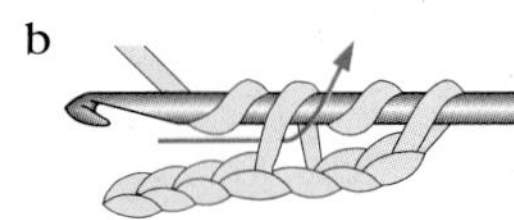

c

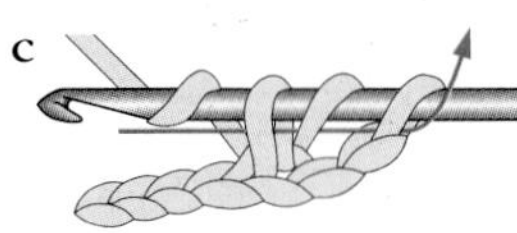

Front Loop (a)/ Back Loop (b)

(front lp/back lp)

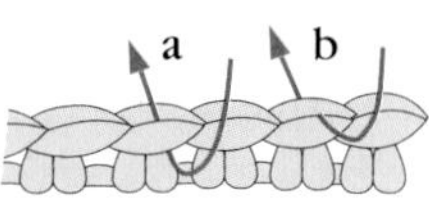

Reverse Single Crochet (reverse sc)

Working from left to right, insert hook in next st to the right (a), yo, draw through st, complete as sc (b).

a

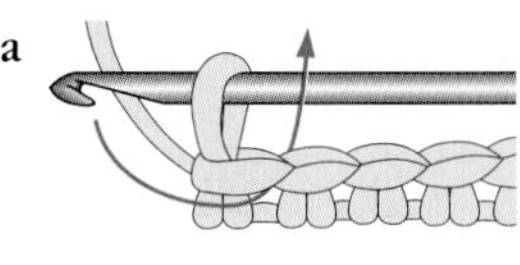

b

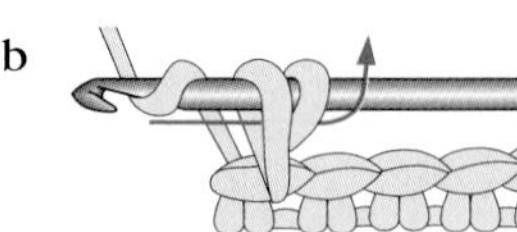

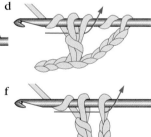

The patterns in this book are written using American crochet stitch terminology. For our international customers, hook sizes, stitches and yarn definitions should be converted as follows:

US	UK
sl st (slip stitch)	= sc (single crochet)
sc (single crochet)	= dc (double crochet)
hdc (half double crochet)	= htr (half treble crochet)
dc (double crochet)	= tr (treble crochet)
tr (treble crochet)	= dtr (double treble crochet)
dtr (double treble crochet)	= ttr (triple treble crochet)
skip	= miss

Thread/Yarns

Bedspread Weight	= No.10 Cotton or Virtuoso
Sport Weight	= 4 Ply or thin DK
Worsted Weight	= Thick DK or Aran

Measurements

1"	= 2.54 cm
1 yd.	= .9144 m
1 oz.	= 28.35 g

But, as with all patterns, test your gauge (tension) to be sure.

Crochet Hooks

Metric	US	Metric	US
.60mm	14	3.00mm	D/3
.75mm	12	3.50mm	E/4
1.00mm	10	4.00mm	F/5
1.50mm	6	4.50mm	G/6
1.75mm	5	5.00mm	H/8
2.00mm	B/1	5.50mm	I/9
2.50mm	C/2	6.00mm	J/10

Double Love Knot Illustration

ep 1:

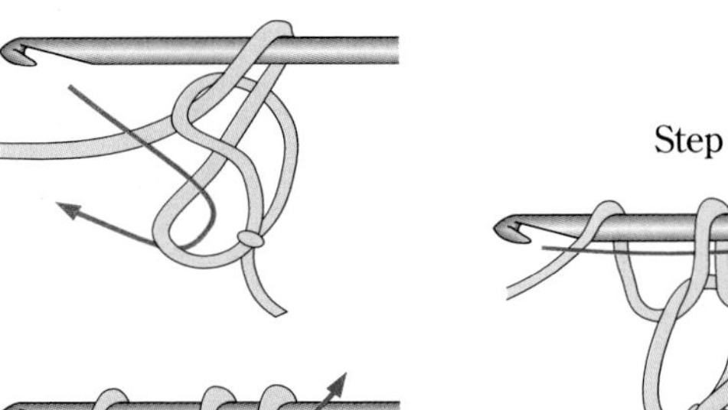

Step 5:

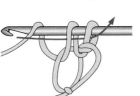

ep 2:

ep 3:

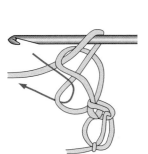

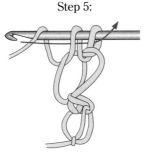

Completed
Double Love Knot

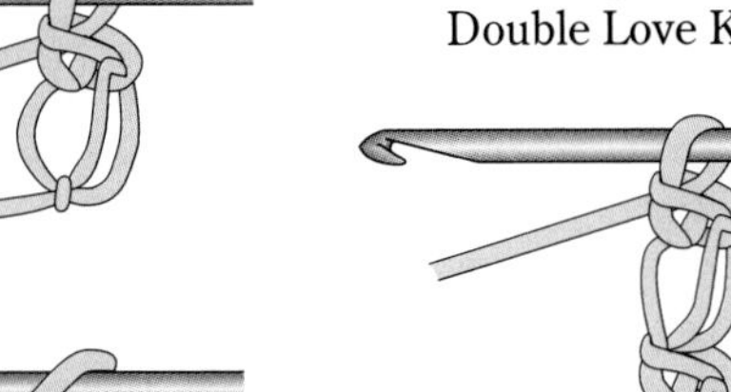

ep 4:

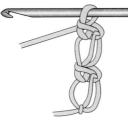

Single Crochet Color Change
(sc color change)
Drop first color; yo with 2nd color, draw through last 2 lps of st.

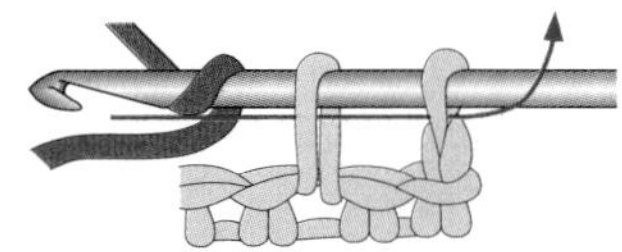

Double Crochet Color Change
(dc color change)
Drop first color; yo with 2nd color, draw through last 2 lps of st.

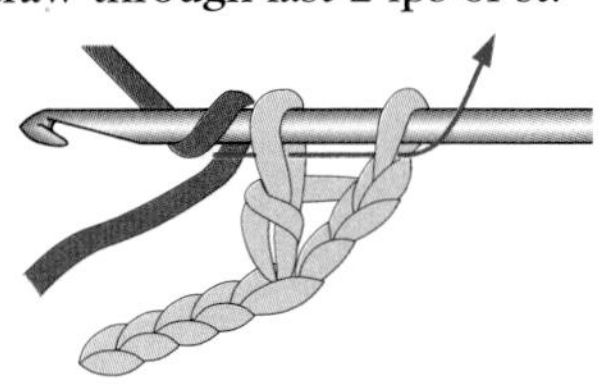

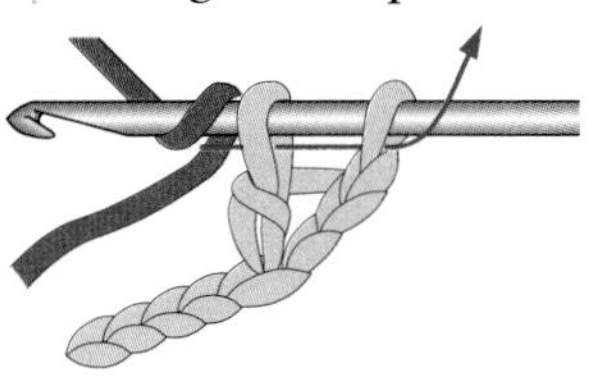

Single Crochet next 2 stitches together
(sc next 2 sts tog)
Draw up lp in each of next 2 sts, yo, draw through all 3 lps on hook.

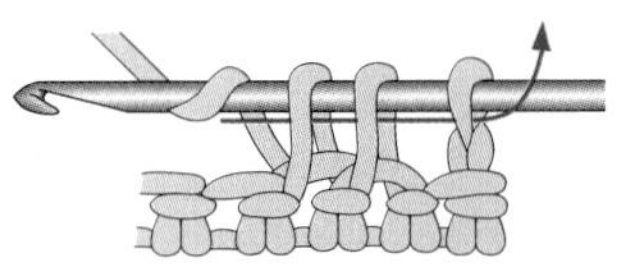

Half Double Crochet next 2 stitches together
(hdc next 2 sts tog)
(Yo, insert hook in next st, yo, draw lp through) 2 times, yo, draw through all 5 lps on hook.

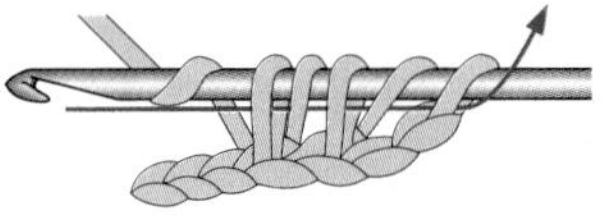

Front Post/Back Post Stitches (fp/bp)
Yo, insert hook from front to back (a) or back to front (b) around post of st on indicated row; complete as stated in pattern.

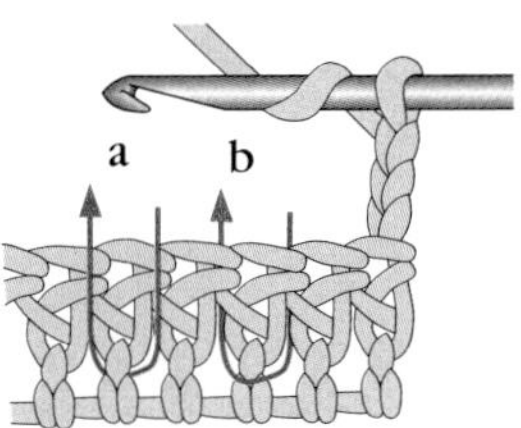

French Knot

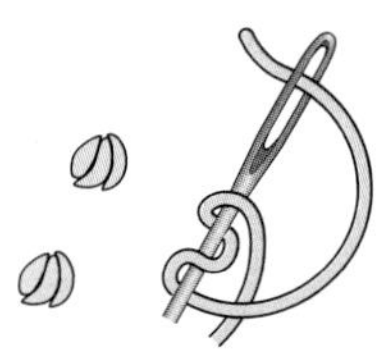

Double Crochet next 2 stitches together
(dc next 2 sts tog)
(Yo, insert hook in next st, yo, draw lp through, yo, draw through 2 lps on hook) 2 times, yo, draw through all 3 lps on hook.

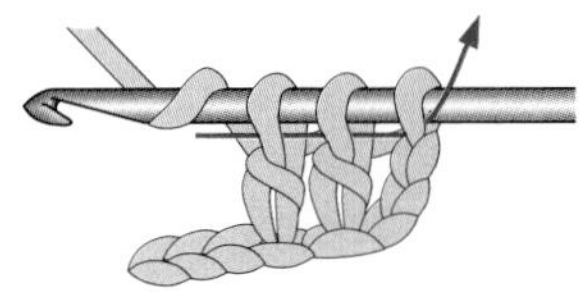

Standard Stitch Abbreviations

ch(s)	chain(s)
dc	double crochet
dtr	double treble crochet
hdc	half double crochet
lp(s)	loop(s)
rnd(s)	round(s)
sc	single crochet
sl st	slip stitch
sp(s)	space(s)
st(s)	stitch(es)
tog	together
tr	treble crochet
tr tr/ttr	triple treble crochet
yo	yarn over

Skill Level Requirements:

★ Easy – Requires knowledge of basic skills only; great for beginners or anyone who wants quick results.

★ ★ Average – Requires some experience; very comfortable for accomplished stitchers, yet suitable for beginners wishing to expand their abilities.

★ ★ ★ Advanced – Requires a high level of skill in all areas; average stitchers may find some areas of these patterns difficult, though still workable.

★ ★ ★ ★ Challenging – Requires advanced skills in both technique and comprehension, as well as a daring spirit; some areas may present difficulty for even the most accomplished stitchers.

Index

Acknowledgments

Our sincere thanks and appreciation to the following yarn companies for graciously providing their products for use in producing this book.

Caron International
Perfect Match - Forest Path
Simply Soft - Floral Hexagon
Wintuk - Forest Path, Grape Vineyard, Victorian Blues

Coats & Clark
Patons Decor - Delightful Daffodils, String of Hearts
Red Heart Classic - Blessed Moments
Red Heart Soft - Butterscotch & Caramel, Indian Harvest, Midsummer Nights, Princess Patchwork, Ribbons and Roses
Red Heart Super Saver - Christmas Senses, Country Rose, Granny's Rose Trellis, Grape Jelly, Ice Cream Cones,Loving Warmth, Magical Night, Moonlit Lane

Lion Brand
Jamie - Baby's Color Wheel
Jiffy - Baby Baubles
Imagine - Blush Rose
Terryspun - Pansies

Spinrite
Bernat Berella 4 - Autumn Splendor, Black-Eyed Susan, Eagle's Ballad, Fall Prisms, Redwork Hearts
Bernat Cherished - Lollipops
Bernat Silky Soft - Braided Sage, Old-Fashioned Christmas
Bernat Softee - Sweet Baby Kisses